THE ALGORITHMIC INSURER

How AI Is Transforming Authority, Accountability and Decision Making in Insurance

DR. IBRAHIM HIKMAT KARAM
Professional Doctorate in Insurance and Risk Management

AI can calculate risk. But who gives it the authority to decide?

SELECTED BOOKS BY THE AUTHOR

Dr. Ibrahim Hikmat Karam has also written:

The Insurance Compass

A Complete Guide to the Insurance Broker Discipline in the GCC and Middle East

The Insurance Constitution

Governing Risk in a Systemic World

Insurance Without Claims

Redesigning Insurance Around Resilience, Not Indemnity

Insurance Risk Ecosystem Entanglement

Understanding Connected Risks. Building Systemic Resilience.

When prediction becomes authority, technology becomes governance.

This book starts from a different place: not with the insurance market we inherited, but with the authority we are beginning to delegate.

FIRST EDITION

The analysis, frameworks, scoring tools, governance models, and policy proposals presented in this book reflect the professional and scholarly judgement of the author. They are offered as educational, governance, and research material and are not legal, actuarial, regulatory, investment, or technology advice. Readers should seek appropriate professional counsel for jurisdiction-specific obligations.

Public case studies are based on publicly available regulatory, judicial, academic, and corporate materials and are identified as such. Composite cases are clearly labelled and are designed to illustrate governance principles without identifying confidential parties.

DEDICATION

For the professionals who will inherit an insurance industry increasingly shaped by machines, and who must ensure that:

- Speed never becomes a substitute for judgement,
- Prediction never becomes a substitute for fairness, and
- Automation never becomes an excuse for the absence of accountability.

AUTHOR'S NOTE

Insurance has always been a decision business disguised as a risk business.

A policy exists because someone decided that a risk was acceptable. A premium exists because someone decided what that risk was worth. A claim is paid because someone decided that an event falls within the promise made by a contract. A reserve is established because someone decided what an uncertain future obligation is likely to become. A portfolio is reinsured because someone decided how much volatility an institution is prepared to carry.

For most of insurance history, those decisions were visibly human. They could be challenged, debated, documented, escalated, defended, and, when necessary, attributed to a person with authority.

That visibility is disappearing.

Today, an insurer may use a model to select a customer, price a policy, flag a claim, estimate damage, recommend a settlement, detect fraud, route a complaint, decide which customer receives a retention offer, or determine which risk should be referred to a human underwriter. Increasingly, the most consequential feature of the decision is not that a machine contributed to it. It is that the machine may determine what the human sees, what the human does not see, and how much practical freedom remains for the human to disagree.

I began writing this book because the same practical problem kept appearing in places that did not fit comfortably inside a technology policy. A tool could be technically sound, legally deployable, and commercially attractive, yet the basic question remained unsettled: who had been given authority, and who would answer when that authority produced harm? That question is narrower than the future of AI, but deeper than model validation. It is the question this book follows.

I am grateful to the insurance professionals, regulators, board members, technologists, actuaries, claims specialists, brokers, risk managers, academics, and clients whose questions have sharpened my thinking over the years. Some were enthusiastic about AI. Some were deeply sceptical. Both groups improved this work. Enthusiasm without governance produces recklessness. Scepticism without curiosity produces irrelevance. The future will belong to institutions capable of combining technological ambition with disciplined accountability.

My deepest gratitude remains with my family, whose support has sustained every professional and scholarly endeavour that preceded this book.

TABLE OF CONTENTS

FIGURES AND TABLES

When Judgement Leaves the Room

Imagine a life insurance applicant sitting at home on a Tuesday evening.

She has not met an underwriter. No medical examiner has visited. She answers a series of questions online and consents to the use of several digital data sources. Within seconds, the system returns a decision. The application is accepted, but at a premium materially higher than she expected.

She asks why.

The customer-service agent sees a screen containing a score, several model-generated factors, and a suggested explanation. The agent did not make the decision. The underwriter did not make the decision. The data scientist who built the model does not know this applicant. The external vendor supplying part of the data cannot disclose its full methodology because it is proprietary. The board has approved an AI policy but has never seen this specific model. The regulator can request documentation, but the consumer wants an answer now.

Who decided?

That question is the beginning of this book.

A Moment From My Own Practice

I did not arrive at this subject by watching technology from a distance. While building an AI-enabled broking platform in Dubai, I kept encountering a practical question that was more difficult than the coding: where should the system stop? We could automate document intake, reconcile insurer data, rank matches, generate comparisons, and prepare the next action. Technically, each additional step was possible. Professionally, possibility was not the same as permission. The moment a workflow could post an allocation, release a commission, recommend an insurer, or move a policy toward binding, the conversation changed from efficiency to authority.

That experience changed how I think about automation. I became less interested in whether a model was impressive and more interested in who could interrupt it, what evidence remained after it acted, and whether a human approval was real or ceremonial. The framework in this book grew from that discomfort as much as from the literature.

The answer cannot be "the algorithm." An algorithm is not a legal person, a professional, a fiduciary, a director, an insurer, or a moral agent. It cannot accept accountability. It cannot be disciplined by a professional body. It cannot be cross-examined in any meaningful human sense. It cannot feel the weight of a decision that leaves a family uninsured, delays a claim after a catastrophe, or incorrectly labels a customer as suspicious.

Yet the phrase "the algorithm decided" is becoming ordinary language. That should concern us.

The central argument of *The Algorithmic Insurer* is simple:

> **Artificial intelligence becomes a governance problem at the moment prediction becomes authority.**

There is nothing inherently improper about an algorithm predicting loss, detecting patterns, summarising files, estimating repair cost, or ranking cases for review. Insurance has used mathematical models for centuries. The governance challenge changes when model output moves from *informing* a professional to *determining* an outcome.

That movement is already occurring. The United States National Association of Insurance Commissioners reports widespread present or planned use of AI and machine learning across auto, homeowners, life, and health insurance. The Bank of England and Financial Conduct Authority found that three quarters of surveyed financial firms were already using AI in 2024, with third-party implementations representing a substantial share of use cases. European insurance supervision now treats AI governance as a distinct risk-management issue, while the European Union's AI Act classifies certain uses in life and health insurance as high-risk. Australia has warned of a potential gap between accelerating AI adoption and slower-moving governance arrangements. Singapore's FEAT principles and Veritas work have attempted to translate fairness, ethics, accountability, and transparency into operational practice.

The regulatory language differs. The underlying problem does not.

The machine is moving closer to the decision.

This book does not argue that humans are inherently fairer, more accurate, or more transparent than algorithms. They are not. Human underwriting can be inconsistent. Human claims decisions can be biased. Human salespeople can discriminate. Human experts can become overconfident, fatigued, politically influenced, or commercially pressured. One of the strongest arguments for algorithmic decision systems is precisely that they can make patterns visible and decisions more consistent.

The relevant choice is therefore not human good, machine bad.

The choice is between governed decision authority and ungoverned decision authority.

A well-designed algorithmic system can be more accountable than a poorly governed human process. A badly designed algorithm can industrialise error at a speed no human bureaucracy could match.

The objective is not to stop automation. It is to decide what should be automated, under what conditions, with what evidence, subject to what limits, and with whose authority.

That requires a governance framework built specifically for insurance.

This book develops that framework.

How to Use This Book

Read it sequentially for the full argument: the chapters build from what an insurance decision actually is, through the way artificial intelligence changes the locus of authority, to what boards, regulators, and professionals should expect from an algorithmic insurance system. Use it as a reference if you already work with AI. Chapter 3 introduces the Governance Test, a set of questions a board, executive, or control function can use immediately, and every chapter of Part Four ends with one. Everything else varies with the material: some chapters carry a documented public case, some a first-person account, some a worked example, and some none at all. Sources sit in Appendix I. The templates, scoring instruments, questionnaires, and dashboards sit in Appendices A to H, in a form that can be lifted directly into an institution.

THE ARGUMENT IN TEN CLAIMS

The argument rests on ten claims. Some extend established research on automation and human judgement; others are propositions I believe insurance has not yet taken seriously enough.

Proposition 1, Authority Displacement

AI risk rises non-linearly when a system moves from producing information to exercising practical decision authority.

Proposition 2, Consequence Before Complexity

Governance intensity should be determined primarily by the consequence of a decision, not by how technically sophisticated the model appears.

Proposition 3, The Proxy Problem

A variable can be predictive and still be normatively unacceptable. Accuracy does not establish fairness, legality, or legitimacy.

Proposition 4, The Human-in-the-Loop Illusion

Human oversight is not meaningful merely because a person can theoretically override a machine. Oversight is real only if the person has time, information, competence, authority, and institutional permission to disagree.

Proposition 5, Outsourcing Does Not Transfer Accountability

An insurer may outsource data, code, cloud infrastructure, or model development. It cannot outsource responsibility for the insurance decision made in its name.

Proposition 6, Dynamic Models Create Dynamic Governance Duties

A model that changes, learns, is retrained, or is reprompted after deployment cannot be governed only at the point of initial approval.

Proposition 7, Contestability Is a Core Insurance Right

A customer materially affected by an algorithmic insurance decision should have an effective route to challenge the data, reasoning, and outcome.

Proposition 8, Model Monoculture Is a Systemic Risk

When many insurers depend on the same data providers, foundation models, cloud infrastructure, or analytical assumptions, individually sensible automation can create market-wide correlation.

Proposition 9, Reversibility Determines Safe Automation

The easier a decision is to reverse without harm, the more safely it can be automated. Irreversible or time-critical decisions require stronger human authority.

Proposition 10, Human Value Moves to the Boundary

As machines become better at routine decisions, the professional value of humans migrates toward exceptions, ambiguity, ethics, negotiation, empathy, system design, and accountability.

These propositions underpin the **Algorithmic Insurance Governance Model (AIGM)** developed in Part Three.

Figure 1. The path from information to consequence is the organising logic of the book

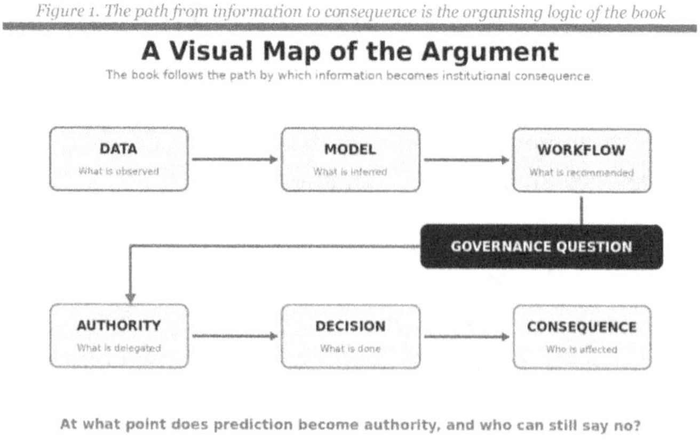

PART I

DECISION

When insurance learns to decide, the most important change is not that insurance can calculate faster. It is that calculation can now become action before a human being has had time to ask whether the action should occur.

CHAPTER 1

Insurance Has Always Been a Decision Machine

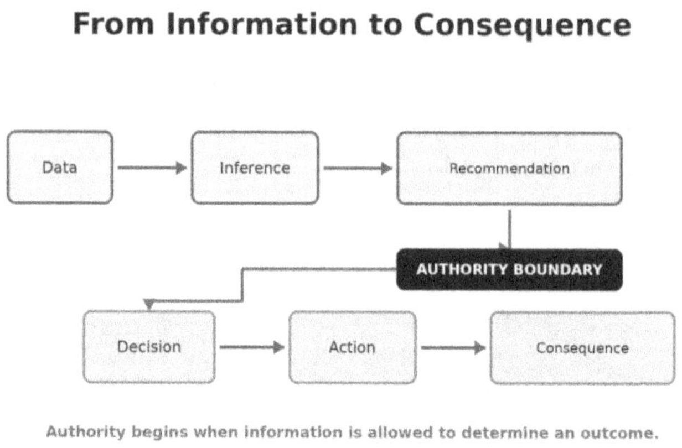

Figure 1.1. From information to consequence.

1.1 Insurance Before Computers

Picture a marine underwriter at Lloyd's in the 1780s. He has no neural network. He has shipping records, a memory for routes and seasons, opinions about particular captains, coffee-house gossip that functions as commercial intelligence, and the scar tissue of past losses. Out of that incomplete material he produces an answer to a question the industry still asks every hour of every day: on what terms should I accept this risk?

Strip away two and a half centuries of technology and the work is recognisably the same work modern machine learning performs. Take incomplete information about the past and present; make a structured judgement about an uncertain future. The technology has changed beyond recognition. The architecture of the decision has barely changed at all, and it is worth setting out, because everything else in this book stands on it.

Every insurance decision contains four layers. Observation: what facts and signals are available. Interpretation: what those facts mean

for risk. Judgement: what outcome is justified. Action: what the insurer will actually do. The Lloyd's underwriter carried all four layers inside one head, which had a governance property nobody appreciated until it was gone: the layers could not drift apart. Modern insurance separates them. Data platforms observe. Models interpret. Workflow systems recommend. Administration systems execute. The separation is what makes insurance fast, and it is also what makes accountability hard to see.

The difference shows the moment something goes wrong. If a senior underwriter misprices a large industrial risk, the organisation can pull the file, reconstruct the judgement, check the authority limit, and ask what she knew at the time. If a machine-driven workflow misprices ten thousand risks, the answer is distributed across a data vendor, a feature pipeline, a model trained six months earlier, a calibration rule, a pricing engine, and an automated deployment. The decision still happened. Responsibility has been sliced thin enough to be invisible.

1.2 Models Are Not New

Insurance is full of models that nobody calls artificial intelligence. Mortality tables are models. Catastrophe models are, obviously, models. The generalised linear models under motor pricing, the credit scores in premium finance, reserving techniques, fraud rules: all models. Even an underwriting manual is a model written in prose. If condition A is present, require information B. If threshold C is exceeded, refer to authority D.

So the novelty of AI is not that insurers have started modelling. The novelty lies in four characteristics that increasingly arrive together. Scale: the system can process more data and more decisions than human teams could realistically review. Complexity: the relationship between input and output resists ordinary business explanation. Adaptivity: the system changes after deployment, through retraining, new prompts, new data, or automated optimisation. And execution: the output can be wired directly into operational systems, so that prediction becomes action with no one in between.

Only the fourth is decisive for governance, and I want to be plain about why. A model that predicts the probability of claims fraud and leaves the investigator fully responsible for the next step is one kind of thing. A model that automatically freezes payment, routes the customer to a special investigation unit, and writes a fraud marker that will follow that customer into future underwriting is another kind of thing entirely. The prediction may be identical in both cases. The authority is not, and authority, not sophistication, is what this book is about.

1.3 The Wrong Starting Question

Most organisations begin AI governance by asking what counts as AI. The instinct is understandable. Regulation needs definitions, inventories need scope, and technology teams need categories. For insurance governance it is nonetheless the wrong first question, and starting there costs organisations a year they do not get back.

Here is why. A simple rule can do more harm than an advanced model. A deterministic pricing engine that silently declines every applicant above a threshold has more consequence than a sophisticated language model that summarises policy documents for an underwriter to read. Chase the definition and you will spend months debating whether the first system is "really AI" while it declines applicants unexamined, and heavy governance will land on the harmless summariser because it carries the fashionable label.

Governance should begin with a different question: what decision is being made, who is affected, and how much practical authority has been delegated to the system? This book calls that starting point decision-first governance. It does not ignore technical complexity; it puts complexity in the correct order.

First understand the decision. Then understand the machinery that supports it.

In Practice: Progressive Snapshot

Usage-based motor insurance shows how a data source can quietly change the meaning of a traditional underwriting variable. Progressive's Snapshot programme collects driving information, speed, time of day, phone use, acceleration and braking, and other derived behavioural measures, depending on programme and device. The old underwriting question, what kind of driver is this, was once answered by age, vehicle, location, and claims history. Now it can be answered by watching the driving. The governance lesson is not that telematics is good or bad. It is that one new data source changed three things at once: what the insurer can know, how often it can know it, and how closely the premium can follow behaviour. A decision that once ran on broad categories can become individualised and continuous. The more granular the observation, the heavier the load on consent, relevance, proportionality, error correction, and the increasingly thin line between risk measurement and surveillance.

1.4 The Decision Is the Unit of Governance

Traditional model governance treats the model as the unit of analysis. Has it been validated? Is performance within tolerance? Is the documentation complete? Those questions remain necessary and this book assumes they are being asked. They are no longer sufficient, for one stubborn reason: the same model can be low-risk in one context and dangerous in another.

A language model drafting internal meeting notes is not the same governance object as the identical model generating coverage advice for customers. A fraud model prioritising files for review is not the same object as the identical model denying claims on its own. A computer vision model estimating vehicle damage for an adjuster to check is not the same object as the identical model issuing final settlements. In each pair, nothing about the mathematics has changed. Everything about the consequence has. The correct governance object is therefore the AI-enabled decision system: the complete chain from data input through model output to operational consequence.

Govern the chain and the model comes with it. Govern only the model and the chain will surprise you.

CHAPTER 2

From Actuarial Model to Artificial Intelligence

2.1 Four Generations of Decision Technology

The history of insurance analytics compresses into four generations. Rules and tables came first: mortality tables, rating factors, underwriting manuals, authority grids, deterministic claims rules, systems that apply predetermined relationships. Statistical prediction followed, estimating relationships from data while staying broadly interpretable; the generalised linear models, credibility methods, and traditional fraud scores of the actuarial mainstream live here. Machine learning came third, finding patterns too tangled for simple rules to express: gradient boosting, random forests, neural networks, computer vision. The fourth generation is generative and agentic. These systems do not only classify or predict. They produce content, reason across instructions and documents, hold conversations, call tools, and increasingly take sequences of actions toward an objective.

The generations do not replace each other; they stack. A single claim today can be routed by a Generation One rule, scored by a Generation Three model, summarised by a Generation Four language model, and paid by an automated workflow. Which is why the label "AI" misleads more than it informs. The governance challenge is never the label. It is the chain.

2.2 Training and Inference Without the Mystery

Machine learning is routinely described in vocabulary that excludes the very executives who must govern it, and the exclusion is unnecessary. The working concepts fit in a paragraph.

Training is the process by which a model adjusts itself to patterns in historical or synthetic examples. Inference is what happens when the trained model receives a new input and produces an output. For generative AI, a prompt supplies instructions and context, and the model predicts the sequence of words most likely to follow; the result can be impressive, useful, and wrong, in any combination. An agentic system adds one more layer: the model can select tools, retrieve information, act, evaluate what happened, and continue until it reaches an objective or a stopping condition.

Each layer carries its own governance question. Training raises data quality, bias, representativeness, and the choice of target. Inference raises accuracy and stability. Prompting raises instruction control and context leakage. Tool use raises permissions. Autonomy raises authority. A director who can keep those five pairings straight understands enough to govern; most of what lies deeper is the model team's job, not the board's.

2.3 Why Generative AI Is Different

A traditional pricing model produces a bounded output: a score, a probability, a factor, a price indication. If it fails, it usually fails visibly, with a number strange enough to trigger a question. A generative model fails differently. It can produce language that carries the full tone of professional certainty while being wrong, and nothing about the sentence warns you.

This matters more in insurance than in almost any other industry, because insurance is made of language. Policy interpretation, coverage explanation, claims correspondence, underwriting rationale, complaint responses, broker advice, regulatory reporting, board papers: language tasks, all of them, and until recently every one of them was protected by the slow human machinery of professional writing, review, and sign-off. A system that writes convincingly walks straight past that protection. The deep risk is not hallucination as such. It is institutional confidence in plausible language: the polished paragraph nobody thought to check, because polish is what checking used to look for.

2.4 The New Model Risk: Behaviour

Traditional model risk asks whether the model is mathematically sound, calibrated, stable out of sample, and free of drift. Generative and agentic systems add a stranger set of questions, closer to personnel management than to statistics. Does it follow instructions consistently? Can it be manipulated through prompt injection? Does it invent information when evidence is missing? Does it leak confidential data? Does it answer differently when the same request is worded differently? Can it reach tools beyond its intended permissions, or assemble a chain of actions that no single control owner anticipated?

Notice what has happened to the object under governance. The model is no longer only a statistical artefact to be validated. It is a behavioural component inside an operational system, and a reputable brand name on the box settles none of the questions above; a third-party model arrives pre-trained, not pre-validated for your decisions. Later chapters build the machinery for governing behaviour. The point here is simply that the category exists.

2.5 Literacy Without Pretence

Boards respond to technological complexity in two unhelpful ways. The first is delegation: the technology team understands it, so the board need not. The second is theatre: directors attend a half-day workshop and are minuted as AI literate. I have more sympathy for the second failure than the first, since it at least admits the obligation, but neither survives contact with a real incident.

Here is the standard that actually matters. A board does not need to understand backpropagation, any more than an audit committee needs to derive the discount curve. It does need to hold five distinctions firmly: prediction versus decision, closed model versus third-party service, static tool versus agent, validation versus monitoring, and theoretical oversight versus practical human authority. That is governance literacy. It fits on one page, it can be tested in ten minutes of questioning, and a board that has it will ask better questions than a board of lapsed programmers.

CHAPTER 3

When Prediction Becomes Authority

3.1 The Authority Boundary

Suppose a fraud model assigns a claim a risk score of 0.82. That number, by itself, denies nothing. It accuses no one and delays no payment. It is information, and information can be governed with the tools insurance has always had.

Now suppose the claims system automatically routes every score above 0.80 into an investigation queue, suspends payment, and sends the customer a standard letter. Nothing about the model has changed. The mathematics is identical, the score is identical, and yet everything that matters has changed, because the output has acquired consequence. A customer is now waiting for money on the strength of a threshold someone set in a configuration file.

This book calls that crossing point the Authority Boundary, and the sentence worth carrying out of this chapter is short: the boundary is crossed not when a model becomes sophisticated but when its output acquires consequence. Every insurer using AI should be able to say, for every material process, exactly where the Authority Boundary sits. Most cannot, and the rest of this chapter explains why the honest answer is harder to produce than it looks.

3.2 Formal Authority and Practical Authority

Organisations describe a process as human-controlled because a human retains formal authority. The underwriter can override the model. The claims manager can reverse the fraud flag. The service agent can escalate past the chatbot. All true, all documented, and all potentially worthless.

Consider a claims examiner receiving three hundred model-scored files a day. The system ranks them, supplies a recommended outcome, highlights the facts it considers relevant, and measures her handling time. She retains discretion in every formal sense. In practice, disagreeing means opening another workflow, writing a justification, and perhaps waiting for a supervisor, while the accept button sits one click away and the clock on her dashboard runs. The machine has been given no legal authority whatsoever. It has acquired something more useful: workflow authority, the authority that comes from making agreement cheap and disagreement expensive.

Workflow authority is among the most important ideas in this book, because it explains a pattern that otherwise looks paradoxical: organisations with impeccable human-in-the-loop policies whose humans, measurably, never disagree with the loop.

From Practice: The Approval That Had to Mean Something

In our own broking operation, one of the most revealing automation problems appeared in finance rather than underwriting. Producer commission can look mechanically simple: identify the policy, identify the amount due, and post the allocation. In reality, we imposed a harder rule. A producer should not be paid simply because the policy exists. The client premium must have been collected and the insurer commission must have been received. Those conditions are commercial, accounting, and governance conditions at the same time.

When we automated the workflow, I insisted on two separate approvals: first the brokerage allocation, then the producer payment. The system checks voucher references, allocation IDs, available balances, and duplicate postings, but it does not collapse the two decisions into one. That design costs a few clicks. It also preserves the distinction between a machine finding a payable item and an authorised person deciding that the conditions for payment have actually been met. This is what I mean by practical authority. If the human approval can be skipped without changing the outcome, it is not authority. It is decoration.

3.3 The Human-in-the-Loop Illusion

None of this is new, which is itself worth knowing. Lisanne Bainbridge described the "ironies of automation" in 1983:

automate the routine work and you leave the human with exactly the tasks the machine cannot do, the rare, ambiguous, dangerous ones, while simultaneously eroding the skills and situational awareness the human needs to do them (Bainbridge, 1983). Forty years later, insurers are rediscovering her ironies one deployment at a time. The reviewer we station at the end of the automated pipeline is asked to catch precisely the cases the pipeline could not handle, using judgement the pipeline has given her ever fewer opportunities to practise.

So what would a meaningful human decision actually require? Five conditions. Time: enough to review the case rather than ratify it. Information: access to evidence beyond what the model chose to display. Competence: the professional knowledge to recognise when the model may be wrong. Authority: permission to override without disproportionate escalation. Independence: incentives that do not punish disagreement for being slower than agreement. Remove any one of the five and "human oversight" continues to exist on the organisation chart while having quietly ceased to exist anywhere else.

3.4 Automation Bias, and Its Opposite

Humans over-rely on automated recommendations, especially when the system is presented as accurate, scientific, or data-driven; the literature on types and levels of automation has documented the effect across aviation, medicine, and process control for decades (Parasuraman, Sheridan and Wickens, 2000). Insurance adds its own accelerant: workload. The danger is not that professionals become lazy. It is that organisations redesign processes around the expectation that the machine is usually right, and once performance targets are calibrated to automated throughput, careful disagreement becomes operationally expensive. Accepting the model is easy; challenging it is costly. I call this automation asymmetry, and in high-consequence decisions the explicit job of governance is to reverse it: make justified override easy, measurable, and professionally legitimate.

Honesty requires the other half of the research, too. People also exhibit algorithm aversion: shown a model making an occasional error, they abandon it, even when it still outperforms the humans who replaced it (Dietvorst, Simmons and Massey, 2015). Both failure modes are real. A workforce can rubber-stamp the model on Monday and distrust it into uselessness on Friday, and the difference is usually a memorable recent error. The governance implication is that neither a high override rate nor a low one is good news in itself. What matters is whether disagreement, when it happens, is justified, and whether justified disagreement is possible at all. That is what the next section measures.

In Practice: AI Underwriting at Industrial Scale

Ping An reported that in the first half of 2025, 94 per cent of its life insurance policies were underwritten within seconds, and AI representatives handled roughly 80 per cent of customer service volume. Commercially, the figures are formidable. For this chapter they are something else: a demonstration that the question "should a human review this decision?" has already been answered by arithmetic. At second-level underwriting speed there is no version of universal manual review. Governance at that scale cannot live in the review step, because there is no review step. It has to be built into the architecture: which cases are eligible for automation at all, what triggers referral, how exceptions are detected, how outcomes are monitored across segments, and how a customer challenges an adverse result. The objective is not to slow every decision down to human speed. It is to draw the boundary between automated scale and human authority deliberately, rather than letting throughput draw it.

3.5 Effective Disagreement

The strongest test of human oversight is not whether a human can approve a machine recommendation. Approval is cheap. The test is whether a human can disagree effectively, and effectiveness leaves evidence an organisation can measure: override rates and the reasons behind them; whether overrides improve outcomes; whether particular teams never disagree at all; whether disagreement is concentrated among senior staff, which usually means junior staff have learned not to try; whether the people who override are quietly penalised through productivity metrics; and whether the model is actually updated when justified disagreement forms a repeated pattern. Override is not a failure of automation. It is the system's proof of life.

The Governance Test: The Effective Disagreement Test A human-in-the-loop arrangement is credible only if the answer to all five questions is yes:

1. **Can the human see the evidence needed to challenge the recommendation?**

2. **Can the human override without disproportionate delay or permission?**

3. **Is there enough time to exercise judgement?**

4. **Are overrides monitored as learning signals rather than treated as productivity failures?**

5. **Can the customer reach a human reviewer when the outcome materially affects**

3.6 The Control Room Problem: Oversight Under Pressure

The hardest oversight problem never appears in a policy document. It appears at 4:45 in the afternoon, when a reviewer has twenty-seven files left, the system's historical acceptance rate is 92 per cent, and the dashboard on the wall rewards speed. On paper, the human retains authority. In practice, the workflow decided hours ago how expensive disagreement would be.

I call this the control room problem. Governance tends to be designed as though humans meet machine recommendations in seminar conditions, rested and unhurried. Real insurance work is claims teams against service standards, underwriters against quote deadlines, fraud teams against queues, service staff measured on handling time. The practical authority of an algorithm is therefore set partly by things no model document mentions: queue design, screen layout, escalation permissions, staffing levels, and what happens to the reviewer who overrides. Can she see contradictory evidence without opening six systems? Is the reason for the recommendation visible before the accept button, or only after? Does an override trigger a coaching conversation or a disciplinary one? Those answers, not the AUC, decide whether oversight is a control or a fiction.

Supervisors are converging on the same view. The IAIS emphasises governance, accountability, human oversight, transparency, and redress; EIOPA's 2025 Opinion treats human oversight as part of a risk-based governance system rather than a decorative final step (IAIS, 2025; EIOPA, 2025). The implication deserves italics somewhere: meaningful human authority has to be engineered into the decision environment before deployment. And the Effective Disagreement Test must be run in production-like conditions, because a reviewer who overrides comfortably in a workshop may be unable to do so under real load. Test the system people actually work in, not the one drawn in the process map.

CHAPTER 4

The Algorithmic Insurance Value Chain

4.1 AI Is Not One Use Case

People discuss "AI in insurance" as though it were one technology with one risk profile. Walk the value chain and the phrase dissolves. At the front, AI generates leads, segments customers, triages quotes, and answers chat. In the core, it extracts documents, supports underwriting, prices risk, detects fraud, estimates damage, recommends reserves, settles claims, and handles complaints. Around the edges it summarises calls, drafts policy language, supports brokers, analyses reinsurance, monitors catastrophes, and writes software. It has even reached the control functions, where it tests compliance, assists internal audit, and drafts the board papers that are supposed to govern it.

These uses are nowhere near equally consequential, and three contrasts make the gradient visible. A model summarising a claims file for an adjuster is different from a model determining whether the claim is covered. A system recommending marketing content is different from one deciding whether a policy renews. A model that assists internal audit is different from a model whose output is itself accepted as audit evidence. Same technology family in each pair; entirely different governance object.

4.2 Three Zones of AI Use

For governance purposes, uses divide into three zones. Zone One is productivity AI: tools that help people work faster without materially determining customer or risk outcomes. Drafting, summarisation, internal search, code assistance, meeting notes. Zone Two is decision support: tools that influence judgement. Underwriting scores, fraud alerts, severity estimates, claim recommendations. Zone Three is decision authority: tools that determine or execute outcomes.

Automated acceptance and declinature, pricing, claim payment, customer communication, cancellation.

The essential subtlety is that zones are not properties of models. They are properties of integration. The same language model is Zone One while it drafts internal notes, Zone Two the day someone pipes its summaries into underwriting screens, and Zone Three the week its output starts populating customer letters that go out unread. Nothing was retrained. Somebody just connected a wire, and connecting wires rarely goes through model governance. Watching zone migration is therefore one of the register's most important jobs, and the reason inventories go stale.

4.3 Decision Lineage

Every material AI use case should have a documented decision lineage: what data entered the process, which systems transformed it, which model produced the recommendation, which business rule converted recommendation into action, which human roles could intervene, which system executed the outcome, and what evidence was retained afterward.

Seven questions, and answering them sounds like bureaucracy until the day a regulator, a court, or a customer asks why a specific decision happened, and the organisation discovers that the answer is distributed across five systems and two vendors, none of which logged the part it played. Lineage is how accountability survives the very thing that makes automation valuable: the handoffs. Without it, responsibility breaks exactly at the system boundaries where the speed lives.

4.4 The Inventory Problem

The first governance failure in most organisations is not a bad model. It is an incomplete inventory, and the incompleteness is nobody's decision. AI seeps in. A claims vendor activates a feature that did not exist when the contract was signed. A cloud platform adds summarisation to a product the firm already licenses. An employee builds a workflow on a public language model because it is Tuesday and the work is düe Wednesday. A developer integrates an external API into a process and would never think to call it an insurance model.

The surveys confirm what the anecdotes suggest: the Bank of England and FCA found rapid adoption with heavy third-party implementation, and ASIC's review of Australian licensees counted hundreds of AI use cases while warning that governance arrangements risked falling behind them (Bank of England & FCA, 2024; ASIC, 2024). The lesson does not need dressing up. An organisation cannot govern systems it does not know it uses, and every organisation uses systems it does not know about.

4.5 The Algorithmic Register

The remedy is an Algorithmic Register, deliberately broader than a traditional model inventory. Each entry should capture four clusters of information. Identity: system name and version, business purpose, provider, and the decision affected. Accountability: the named owner, the authority level, the consequence classification, and the human oversight mechanism. Substance: data sources, model type, third-party dependencies, and customer disclosure status. And lifecycle: validation date, monitoring metrics, incident history, and the retirement plan, because models leave residue, and a model can be decommissioned while its outputs live on inside downstream rules nobody remembers writing.

Two rules keep a register honest. It should include simple deterministic rules whenever those rules materially automate customer outcomes, because governance cannot depend on whether a technologist chooses to call something "AI." And it should treat vendor product updates as potential model changes, not operational noise, since that is precisely how the hidden feature in the case above got in.

PART II

DATA

What the machine sees is never simply the world. It is a record shaped by earlier choices, missing information, institutional habits, and the purposes for which data was collected.

CHAPTER 5

Data Is Not Neutral

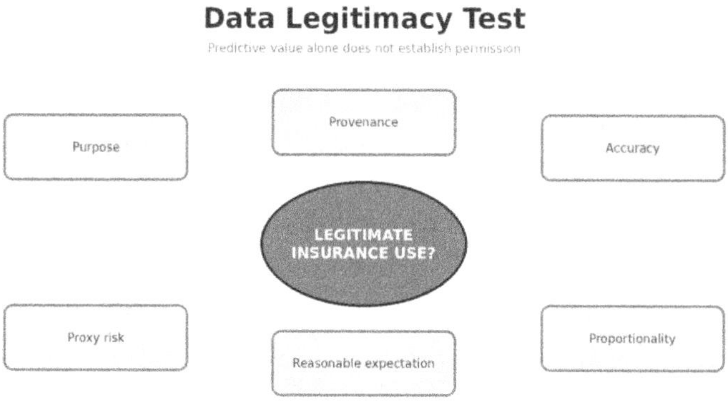

Figure 5.1. The Data Legitimacy Test.

5.1 The Myth of Raw Data

Insurance professionals often speak of "raw data" as if information arrives untouched by human judgement. It does not. A claims file exists because someone decided what to record. A medical code reflects a clinical and administrative system. A credit file reflects rules about who receives credit and which transactions are visible. A motor telematics record reflects the sensors chosen by the provider and the definitions embedded in software. Even a photograph has a viewpoint, a resolution, a timestamp, and a missing world outside the frame.

The first discipline of algorithmic governance is therefore epistemic humility: before asking what a model can learn from a dataset, ask how the dataset came to exist. Insurance is especially vulnerable to forgetting this because the industry has always relied on structured records. Familiarity creates a dangerous assumption that the record is the risk itself. It is not. It is evidence about the risk, filtered through a process.

From Practice: A Screening System Is Not a Control Until Its Settings Are Governed

A Central Bank of the UAE targeted examination of our sanctions framework reinforced this lesson for me in a way no abstract model-risk discussion could. The issue was not whether a screening system existed. It did. The issue was whether its thresholds were formally defined and locked, whether date of birth and nationality were mandatory fields, whether the matching logic was documented, and whether the Board had approved the risk appetite around those decisions. The findings were remediated, but the lesson stayed with me.

A system can be technically operational and still be weakly governed. Data fields, thresholds, ownership and escalation rules are not back-office details. They are part of the decision. The same principle applies to AI. A model does not become trustworthy because the vendor calls it accurate. The institution has to know what data enters, which settings matter, who can change them, and what evidence proves that those choices were authorised.

5.2 Three Questions About Every Dataset

A governance review should distinguish three questions. **Quality** asks whether the data is accurate, complete, timely, and technically usable. **Relevance** asks whether it is genuinely informative about the insured event or decision. **Legitimacy** asks whether it is appropriate to use the information for this purpose, even if it is accurate and predictive.

The third question is the one conventional model governance most often underweights. A variable can predict loss and still be unacceptable because it functions as a proxy for a protected characteristic, because the customer could not reasonably anticipate its use, because it was obtained in a context inconsistent with the insurance purpose, or because its predictive power arises from structural inequality rather than underlying risk. The fact that a variable improves a model is evidence of usefulness, not evidence of legitimacy.

5.3 Labels Are Decisions Frozen in Data

Supervised learning requires a target: a historical outcome the model is asked to predict. In insurance, targets frequently come from earlier human or institutional decisions, claims referred for investigation, applications declined, cases escalated, customers who cancelled, claims classified as suspicious, or files judged complex.

If the historical label was shaped by unequal investigation intensity or inconsistent judgement, the model can reproduce that pattern with greater consistency than the humans ever achieved. This is one reason a model can be statistically impressive while institutionally wrong. It may be excellent at predicting what the organisation used to do rather than what the organisation ought to do.

A model trained to predict "fraud referral" is not necessarily predicting fraud. It may be predicting the historical behaviour of the referral process. That distinction should appear in the model documentation in plain language.

5.4 Provenance as Decision Evidence

Data provenance is the ability to answer where information came from, under what authority it was collected, how it was transformed, what limitations are known, how frequently it changes, and which decisions depend on it. In a modern insurance stack, a single score may be assembled from dozens of sources: proposal data, public records, behavioural data, third-party scores, geospatial layers, device signals, and derived features.

The governance problem is not solved by a data dictionary. Provenance must follow the data into the decision. If a regulator, customer, court, or board asks why a materially adverse outcome occurred, the insurer should be able to reconstruct not merely the final model score but the lineage of material data that contributed to it.

5.5 The Data Legitimacy Test

This book proposes a six-question **Data Legitimacy Test** for any material variable or dataset used in an insurance decision:

1. **Purpose**, Is the information reasonably connected to the insurance purpose for which it is used?
2. **Provenance**, Can the source, transformation history, and ownership be reconstructed?
3. **Accuracy**, Can a materially affected person challenge factual errors?
4. **Proxy risk**, Could the information act as a substitute for a characteristic the institution should not use directly?
5. **Expectation**, Would a reasonable customer understand that this category of information could affect the decision?
6. **Proportionality**, Is the decision benefit sufficient to justify the intrusion, complexity, or potential harm? A dataset that fails the test should not become legitimate merely because model performance declines when it is removed.

5.6 The Cost of Cheap Data

The most dangerous data is often not the obviously sensitive data. It is the inexpensive data that arrives with a polished API, a confident score, and no one in the room who can explain how the underlying facts were created. Cheap data lowers the friction of experimentation, and that is precisely why it can enter consequential decisions before its legitimacy has been examined.

Insurance has always bought external information. Motor records, credit attributes, medical evidence, property characteristics, geospatial layers, sanctions data, repair estimates, catastrophe models, and fraud intelligence are not new. What changes in an AI environment is the volume of sources, the speed with which they can be combined, and the distance between the original fact and the decision that finally uses it. A model may rely on a variable that is itself the output of another model, which relied on inferred data purchased from a third party, which was built from observations the insurer never collected.

The Data Legitimacy Test should therefore include a question that conventional data-quality programmes often miss: what institutional claim are we making when we use this data? Accuracy is one claim. Permission is another. Relevance is another. Fairness is another. A dataset can be accurate and still be inappropriate because the relationship between the information and the insurance decision is too remote, too intrusive, too unstable, or too difficult for the customer to challenge.

Data provenance becomes more important as inference becomes more powerful. A postcode can become a proxy for socio-economic position. Device metadata can become a proxy for lifestyle. Purchase history can become a proxy for health or financial stress. None of those inferences needs to name a protected characteristic to create a protected-class effect. New York DFS explicitly warns that external consumer data can reflect systemic bias and expects insurers to assess proxy relationships and adverse effects when such data is used in underwriting and pricing (NYDFS, 2024).

Procurement should therefore ask more than whether the vendor can deliver the data. The business owner should be able to state why the information is necessary, what decision it changes, what evidence supports the relationship, how long it will be retained, how a customer can correct it, and what happens if the source disappears. The cheapest data can become very expensive once it has been embedded in a decision the institution can no longer explain.

CHAPTER 6

Proxy Discrimination and the Fairness Problem

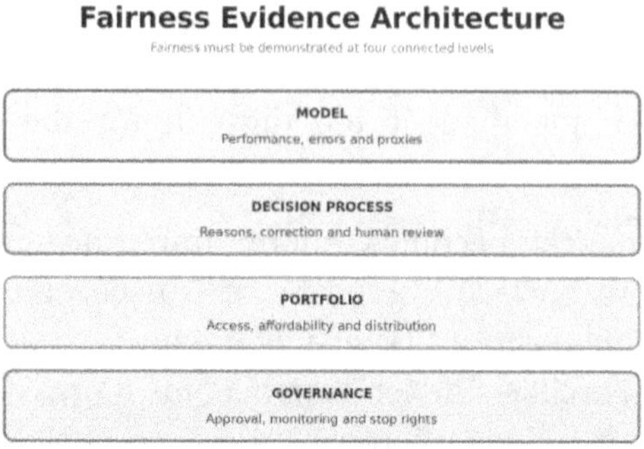

Figure 6.1. Fairness evidence architecture.

6.1 Discrimination Without Naming the Characteristic

A system does not need a field labelled race, religion, disability, or gender to recreate distinctions associated with those characteristics. Postcode, occupation, purchasing behaviour, device type, language, commuting pattern, social network, education, and hundreds of behavioural variables can correlate with protected or vulnerable groups. Modern machine learning is powerful specifically because it finds multivariate relationships too subtle for manual rules. That same capability can make exclusion invisible.

Removing a protected variable is therefore not a sufficient fairness strategy. In some circumstances, it may even make testing harder because the institution loses the ability to detect disparate outcomes. Governance requires a controlled capacity to measure whether decisions are producing unjustified group effects, subject to applicable law and privacy rules.

6.2 Insurance Is Not a Fairness-Free Zone

Insurance legitimately differentiates. A property exposed to greater physical hazard may attract a higher premium. A driver with a materially different expected loss profile may be priced differently. The challenge is that “risk-based” does not end the normative inquiry. Society has always placed boundaries around which differences may justify which insurance consequences.

The relevant question is not whether an algorithm treats everyone identically. It is whether the distinctions it makes are causally and normatively defensible for the insurance purpose, consistent with law, proportionate to the consequence, and supported by evidence rather than convenient correlation.

6.3 Fairness Metrics Do Not Decide Fairness

Technical teams can calculate demographic parity, equalised odds, calibration, error-rate balance, selection ratios, and other measures. These are useful diagnostic tools. They are not moral conclusions. Different fairness measures can conflict, especially when base rates differ. Selecting the metric is therefore a governance decision about what kind of error matters and to whom.

For a fraud triage model, false positives may impose investigation delay and stigma. For a life underwriting model, false negatives and false positives have different commercial and consumer effects. For a claims severity model, the most important question may be whether vulnerable customers systematically receive lower early settlement recommendations. Metrics should follow the decision context.

6.4 External Data Raises the Accountability Bar

External consumer data creates a temptation to treat provenance and fairness as the vendor's problem. Regulators have increasingly rejected that position. New York's insurance guidance makes the principle especially clear: an insurer remains responsible for outcomes arising from third-party data and models used in underwriting or pricing, and vendor confidentiality is not an adequate excuse for inability to explain or assess the result.

This is not merely a regulatory rule. It is basic institutional logic. The customer has a contract with the insurer, not with the invisible supplier three layers down the technology chain.

6.5 The Fairness Evidence Pack

For every high-consequence model, the insurer should maintain a **Fairness Evidence Pack** containing: the decision purpose; affected population; protected and vulnerable groups considered; feature legitimacy review; outcome and error testing; intersectional analysis where lawful and statistically credible; explanation of metric selection; mitigation actions; residual disparity; approval decision; monitoring thresholds; and evidence of redress routes. The pack forces an important shift. Fairness stops being a one-time model-development test and becomes an auditable governance claim.

6.6 Fairness Is a Portfolio Property

Fairness is often discussed as though it can be established by inspecting a model in isolation. Insurance makes that approach especially dangerous. A pricing model may pass a statistical test at policy level while contributing, across a portfolio, to a pattern in which particular communities face systematically higher premiums, narrower coverage, more referrals, or more aggressive fraud scrutiny. The individual model may look neutral while the institution produces an uneven opportunity to obtain protection.

New York's 2024 Circular Letter is instructive because it moves the question from intention to evidence. It expects insurers using artificial intelligence systems and external consumer data in underwriting and pricing to assess disproportionate adverse effects, evaluate proxy relationships, govern third-party models, and remain responsible for outcomes even when the technology is proprietary or externally supplied (NYDFS, 2024). The IAIS takes a similarly outcome-oriented approach, linking fairness with ethics, monitoring, human oversight, and redress (IAIS, 2025).

The practical lesson is that fairness must be assessed at three levels. First is model fairness: how the algorithm treats materially similar cases. Second is decision-process fairness: whether people can understand, challenge, and correct the information used against them. Third is portfolio fairness: whether the accumulation of technically defensible individual decisions changes access to insurance in ways that become socially or regulatorily significant.

These levels can conflict. A more granular model may reduce cross-subsidy and improve technical price adequacy while making insurance unaffordable for a concentrated group. A fraud model may reduce total leakage while sending one population into manual review more often because of a proxy buried in the data. A marketing algorithm may increase conversion while quietly reducing the probability that some customers ever see a suitable product. None of these questions can be resolved by accuracy alone.

For governance purposes, fairness should be treated as an evidence package rather than a moral slogan. The insurer should be able to show what outcome was tested, which groups were compared, why the comparison was relevant, what threshold triggered investigation, what alternative specifications were considered, and who had authority to stop deployment. If those questions cannot be answered, fairness has not been governed; it has merely been asserted.

Table 6.1 The Fairness Evidence Matrix

Evidence layer	Question	Illustrative evidence	Owner
Model	Are materially similar cases treated consistently?	Performance and disparity testing; proxy analysis; sensitivity review	Model owner
Process	Can a person understand and challenge the decision?	Reason codes; data correction route; human review; reversal records	Decision owner
Portfolio	Does the pattern of decisions alter access or affordability?	Distributional monitoring; take-up; declinations; referral rates	Business / conduct
Governance	Who can stop or change the system?	Thresholds; escalation rules; board reporting; assurance findings	Executive / board

Note. The matrix deliberately separates statistical fairness from institutional fairness.

6.7 The Scholarly Foundations of the Proxy Problem

The proxy problem described in this chapter has a substantial scholarly pedigree, and readers who want the deeper argument should know where it lives. The definitive legal treatment is Prince and Schwarcz, who coined the modern framing of proxy discrimination in insurance and demonstrated why anti-discrimination law built around intent fails against models that discover proxies without being told to look (Prince and Schwarcz, 2020). Their central insight anticipates much of this chapter: when a predictive characteristic is causally connected to a protected one, a sufficiently powerful model will find the connection whether or not anyone intends it, and prohibiting the protected variable alone is close to meaningless.

The earlier foundations matter too. Avraham, Logue, and Schwarcz mapped how insurance anti-discrimination law actually varies across states and lines of business, showing that the legal baseline the industry often assumes to be uniform is anything but (Avraham, Logue and Schwarcz, 2014). Swedloff examined what big data risk classification does to the fairness settlement underlying insurance regulation (Swedloff, 2014). On the actuarial side, Frees and Huang provide the discipline's own reckoning with discriminatory pricing, and Barry and Charpentier trace how personalisation changes the mutualisation logic on which insurance was built (Frees and Huang, 2023; Barry and Charpentier, 2020). This book's contribution is not to replace that literature but to convert it into governance machinery: the Fairness Evidence Pack is what an institution builds once it accepts what these scholars proved.

CHAPTER 7

Privacy, Consent, and the Data Exhaust Economy

7.1 From Disclosure to Extraction

Traditional insurance was built around disclosure. The applicant answered questions; the insurer obtained defined records; the contract allocated duties around material information. Algorithmic insurance increasingly operates through extraction and inference. The customer may disclose very little while the system infers a great deal.

A smartphone can reveal movement patterns. A connected car can reveal speed, time of travel, braking, acceleration, and phone interaction. A wearable may reveal activity and sleep patterns. Web behaviour can reveal intent. Transaction data can suggest lifestyle. The governance problem is not simply privacy in the narrow sense of secrecy. It is asymmetry: one party may know increasingly intimate things about the other without the individual understanding what has been inferred or how it affects the price of protection.

7.2 Consent Is Often a Weak Governance Foundation

A long privacy notice followed by an "I agree" button may satisfy a formal requirement in some contexts. It does not necessarily create informed legitimacy. Insurance is not an ordinary digital service because the consequences can involve access to essential financial protection. A person may have little practical bargaining power over data terms when insurance is compulsory, contractually required, or economically necessary.

Governance should therefore ask a stronger question than whether consent exists: *Was the use reasonably foreseeable, proportionate, and connected to the insurance purpose?*

7.3 The Sensitivity of Inference

Raw data can appear benign while the inference is sensitive. Shopping records may predict health conditions. Location patterns may suggest religious observance or union activity. Driving routes may reveal home and work. Typing rhythm can be used as a behavioural identifier. The risk resides in what can be inferred, not only in the category of data collected.

This leads to the principle of **bounded inference**: an insurer should define not only which data it is permitted to collect, but which classes of inference it will and will not derive from that data. A licence to observe should not become an unlimited licence to interpret.

7.4 The Data Bargain Must Create Value Both Ways

Usage-based insurance illustrates a potentially legitimate data bargain. If a driver knowingly shares driving information and receives a clear benefit, personalised feedback, a premium reflecting driving behaviour, safety coaching, or another transparent value, the exchange can strengthen the insurance relationship. If the same data quietly expands into unrelated profiling, the bargain changes.

The ethical sustainability of connected insurance depends on reciprocity. The customer should be able to understand what is collected, why, how it changes the decision, and what value is returned.

7.5 Data Retention Is a Decision Problem

Insurers often justify retaining information because storage is cheap and future analytical value is uncertain. AI reverses that convenience. The more data an institution retains, the more inferences become possible, the more attractive the repository becomes to attackers, and the more difficult it becomes to honour purpose limitation.

Retention policy should therefore be linked to the decision lineage. Data that no longer supports a legitimate business, legal, evidential, or governance purpose should not remain indefinitely simply because future models might find it useful.

In Practice, Telematics and the Visible Bargain

Progressive's Snapshot programme is a useful public example of how data-driven insurance can make the exchange visible. Depending on programme design, driving information can include measures such as speed, hard braking, mileage, time of day, and mobile-phone interaction. The consumer proposition is explicit: driving behaviour may influence the insurance experience and potentially the premium. The governance question is not whether telematics is good or bad. It is whether the boundary stays where the customer was told it would be. If the programme begins as safe-driving assessment and later becomes a source for unrelated eligibility, marketing, or behavioural classification, the insurer has changed the data bargain even if the privacy policy technically permits broad analytics.

7.6 The Secondary Use Problem

Insurance data rarely stays where it was collected. Information gathered to administer a claim becomes evidence at renewal. Photographs taken to assess damage become a property characteristics database. Medical invoices submitted for reimbursement become a health profile. Telematics collected to price motor risk becomes a marketing segmentation variable. Each migration may be individually defensible. Together they change what the customer agreed to without anyone deciding that it should change.

This is the secondary use problem, and it is more difficult in insurance than in most industries because the same institution occupies several roles at once. It administers, it underwrites, it prices, it investigates, it markets, and it renews. Data that moves between those roles has not left the company, so no transfer is recorded, no contract is signed, and no privacy notice is triggered. The movement is invisible precisely because it is internal.

Group and employee benefit schemes concentrate the problem. Claims data submitted so that an employee can be reimbursed may end up informing a renewal negotiation with the employer, a benefit redesign, or a wellness intervention. The employee disclosed in order to obtain a payment. The employer receives an analysis. The distance between those two facts is where governance belongs.

Two controls help. The first is a purpose register: for each material dataset, a record of the purpose for which it was obtained and the purposes for which it may be used, maintained by the business rather than by the technology function. The second is to treat a change of purpose as a change of authority under the Authority Escalation Rule. Moving a dataset from administration into underwriting is not a data project. It is a decision about what the institution knows at the moment it decides.

7.7 Minimisation Belongs in the Model, Not Only the Warehouse

Data minimisation is usually implemented as a retention schedule: how long information is kept and when it is destroyed. That is necessary and insufficient. The more consequential question is not what sits in the warehouse. It is what is allowed to reach the decision.

A model may be trained on hundreds of features when a fraction of them carry most of the predictive weight. Every additional feature is an additional inference the institution has chosen to draw, an additional dependency it has to govern, an additional thing a customer might reasonably want to contest, and an additional route by which a proxy can enter. Feature abundance is rarely a deliberate decision. It is what happens when the pipeline makes adding a variable cheaper than justifying one.

The discipline that helps is a marginal value test applied at feature level. For each material variable, ask what the decision would look like without it and how much worse the outcome would actually be. A variable that improves a metric by a negligible amount while introducing sensitive inference, external dependency, or explanation difficulty is not a free improvement. It is a governance cost the institution has accepted without pricing it.

This test is uncomfortable because it will sometimes conclude that a slightly less accurate model is the better institutional choice. That conclusion is legitimate. Accuracy is one property of a decision system. Explicability, contestability, stability, and proportionality are others, and none of them appears in a validation report unless somebody puts it there.

CHAPTER 8

Generative AI, Synthetic Data, and the Collapse of Provenance

8.1 Prediction Produces a Score; Generation Produces an Apparent Explanation

A conventional pricing model may output a number. A generative model can output a paragraph that sounds like a knowledgeable professional. That linguistic fluency changes behaviour. People are more likely to trust an answer that is coherent, contextual, and confident, even when the underlying evidence is weak.

The risk is not simply "hallucination," a term that can make a serious governance problem sound quirky. In insurance, an invented policy clause, incorrect coverage explanation, fabricated precedent, or inaccurate claims instruction can alter customer behaviour and legal position. When language is part of the service, generated language is operational output.

8.2 Grounding Is More Important Than Eloquence

A generative system used in insurance should be governed according to what it is allowed to know and what evidence it must use. Retrieval-augmented generation can reduce unsupported answers by supplying approved documents as context. It does not eliminate risk. The retrieved document may be outdated, the wrong jurisdiction may be selected, a prompt may omit a critical endorsement, or the model may still combine information incorrectly.

The governance objective is therefore **grounded usefulness**, not conversational elegance. A system that says "I do not have enough verified information to answer" can be more valuable than one that produces a polished but unsupported explanation.

8.3 The Prompt Is Part of the Control Environment

In traditional software, material logic is usually visible in code and configuration. In generative systems, behaviour can change because of system prompts, tool permissions, retrieval sources, model versions, temperature settings, context windows, or user instructions. Prompt governance should therefore be treated as configuration governance.

For material insurance use cases, the organisation should retain approved system prompts, version history, tool access, retrieval corpus, validation scenarios, and evidence of changes. A prompt changed by a product manager on Friday can be as consequential as a code release.

8.4 Synthetic Data: Useful, Not Magical

Synthetic data can help test rare events, protect privacy, balance training sets, and simulate cases that are difficult to obtain. It can also create false confidence. Synthetic records inherit assumptions from the generator. If the generator has never learned a rare but important pattern, producing more synthetic examples may reproduce the absence at greater scale.

Synthetic data should be labelled, lineage-controlled, validated against relevant real-world distributions, and used with explicit knowledge of where it enters the model lifecycle. It is not evidence merely because it resembles evidence.

8.5 Provenance After Generation

For high-consequence generative outputs, provenance should include the user request, system prompt, model and version, retrieved sources, tool calls, output, safety filters, human edits, final action, and timestamp. This creates a **Generation Evidence Record**.

The record should be proportionate. A casual internal brainstorming session does not require litigation-grade logging. A generated declinature letter, coverage explanation, medical summary, or settlement recommendation does.

8.6 When a Fluent System Becomes a Policy Author

Generative systems introduce a subtle change in institutional risk: they do not merely calculate; they speak. A score is usually understood as a machine output. A fluent paragraph is easily mistaken for a reasoned institutional position. That difference matters when a system drafts coverage explanations, claim letters, underwriting rationales, broker communications, or regulatory responses.

The danger is not only hallucination. A generated statement can be factually correct and still be unauthorised. It may combine facts from the wrong jurisdiction, cite a superseded wording, omit a material qualification, or convert an internal hypothesis into an apparently final reason. The more natural the language, the easier it is for the reader to forget that the sentence emerged from probabilistic generation rather than a person exercising delegated authority.

NIST's Generative AI Profile highlights risks including confabulation, information integrity, privacy, security, and human- AI configuration (NIST, 2024). In insurance, these risks interact with contract interpretation. A generated explanation can affect the customer's understanding of what the policy promises even when the underlying claim or underwriting decision remains unchanged.

This creates a simple governance rule: generated language should not be allowed to outrun institutional authority. The organisation must define which sources a system may rely on, what kind of statement it may make, which decisions require approved templates or legal review, when a human must confirm the text, and how the final communication is archived with the evidence that supported it.

The stronger the apparent authority of the message, the stronger the control should be. A chatbot helping a customer locate a document is different from an agent explaining why a claim is excluded. A drafting assistant suggesting neutral wording is different from a system sending a declinature autonomously. The model may be identical. The governance risk is not.

PART III

AUTHORITY

The central problem is not whether a model can predict. It is how much practical authority the institution is prepared to give that prediction, and where human judgement must remain decisive.

CHAPTER 9

The Five Levels of Algorithmic Authority

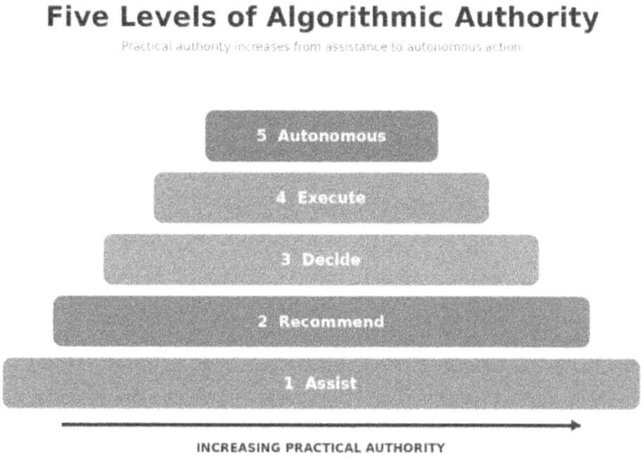

Figure 9.1. Five levels of algorithmic authority.

9.1 The Wrong Classification Question

Boards often begin with labels: machine learning, generative AI, rules engine, predictive analytics, robotic process automation. These labels matter to technical teams, but they are poor first-order governance categories. A simple rule can automatically cancel a policy. A sophisticated language model can merely summarise a meeting. Technical complexity and decision authority are not the same thing.

The **Algorithmic Insurance Governance Model (AIGM)** therefore begins by classifying the authority granted to the system. Authority is observable in workflow: what happens after the output appears?

9.2 Level One, Assist

At **Level One: Assist**, the system performs a task without recommending an insurance outcome. It may extract documents, summarise a file, search approved knowledge, transcribe a call, or draft a note. The human professional retains both informational and decision control.

Level One is not risk-free. A bad summary can omit a crucial exclusion. An extraction tool can misread a sum insured. But the system is not intentionally ranking or directing the insurance decision. Governance should focus on accuracy, confidentiality, access control, and appropriate reliance.

9.3 Level Two, Recommend

At **Level Two: Recommend**, the system proposes an outcome while a human retains practical choice. An underwriting model suggests a loading. A fraud model flags a case. A claims tool proposes reserve range. A customer-service assistant recommends a response.

The critical phrase is *practical choice*. If the human has twenty seconds, cannot see the underlying evidence, is measured on agreement rates, and must write a lengthy justification to disagree, the system may be formally Level Two but effectively Level Three. Authority should be classified by real workflow, not policy language.

9.4 Level Three, Decide

At **Level Three: Decide**, model output determines the outcome unless an exception condition sends the case to a human. Straight-through underwriting, automated fraud disposition, or automatic claim approval can fall here. Human professionals govern the system and exception population, but do not review each ordinary decision.

This level can be highly appropriate for low-consequence, reversible, well-tested decisions. It becomes problematic when "ordinary" is defined by the model itself and edge cases disappear inside confidence scores.

9.5 Level Four, Execute

At **Level Four: Execute**, the system not only determines the decision but carries it into the world: it sends the declinature, transfers the claim payment, changes the premium, initiates cancellation, purchases reinsurance capacity, or modifies a portfolio position.

Execution increases operational consequence because the time between model error and external effect can approach zero. Controls must therefore include transaction limits, pre-execution checks, kill switches, rollback design, and post-execution reconciliation.

9.6 Level Five, Autonomous

At Level Five: Autonomous, the system can pursue an objective across multiple steps, choose tools, adapt plans, interact with other systems, and execute actions with limited case-by-case human direction. Agentic AI makes this level increasingly plausible. An autonomous claims agent might request documents, assess coverage, negotiate a repair booking, approve payment, and communicate with the insured. An autonomous placement agent might analyse exposure, request quotes, compare terms, and negotiate within parameters.

Level Five is not defined by intelligence. It is defined by delegated discretion across a sequence of consequential actions. Governance must therefore control objectives, permissions, boundaries, escalation, memory, counterparties, and the conditions under which autonomy terminates.

9.7 Authority Can Drift

A recurring risk is authority drift. A tool begins as assistance, earns user trust, becomes a recommendation, then is integrated into workflow until recommendations are accepted automatically. No single deployment decision appears revolutionary. The cumulative result is a transfer of authority.

Every material workflow change should therefore reassess the authority level even if the underlying model has not changed.

9.8 The Authority Escalation Rule

The five authority levels become most useful when they are treated as a control ladder rather than a taxonomy. Moving upward should require an explicit governance decision. A system should not become more autonomous simply because users have grown comfortable with it, because a vendor releases a new feature, or because operations teams discover that an additional click can be removed.

The Authority Escalation Rule is therefore: any change that materially reduces human deliberation, narrows the evidence a reviewer sees, increases the share of cases processed without review, adds execution capability, or allows the system to initiate a new action should be treated as an increase in authority even if the underlying model has not changed.

This prevents a common form of governance drift. An organisation validates a recommendation model at Level Two. Months later, the recommendation is pre-selected on screen. Later still, low-value cases are auto-approved unless a reviewer intervenes. Eventually the same workflow executes the decision. No single technology release looked transformational, yet practical authority migrated from Recommend to Execute.

AIGM governance starts by locating the system honestly. The point is not to label the technology sophisticated or unsophisticated. It is to identify how much authority it has, how serious the consequences are, and how entangled the decision is with shared infrastructure, data, models, and downstream actions.

Table 9.1 Five Levels of Algorithmic Authority

Level	Authority	What the system does	Illustrative insurance use
1	Assist	Supplies information; human forms the judgement	Document extraction; policy search
2	Recommend	Suggests an option; human chooses	Referral recommendation; settlement range
3	Decide	Determines the outcome within bounded cases	Low-complexity eligibility or triage decision
4	Execute	Decides and implements the action	Automatic payment, hold, renewal action
5	Autonomous	Initiates and adapts actions with minimal human involvement	Agentic negotiation, dynamic risk action, machine-to-machine placement

CHAPTER 10

The Human Authority Threshold

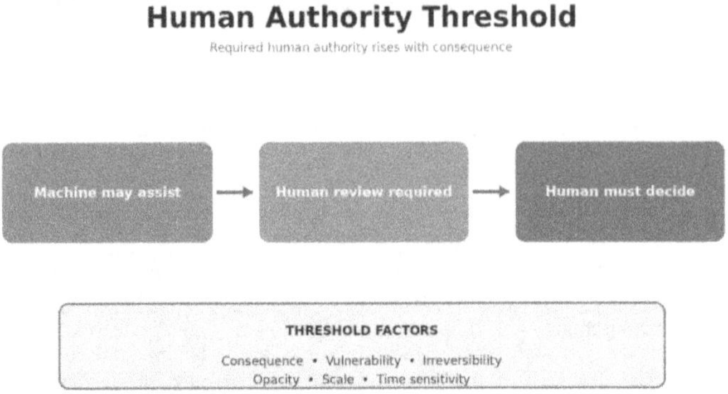

Figure 10.1. The Human Authority Threshold.

10.1 Human Oversight Is a Design Choice

Regulatory and corporate documents frequently promise "human oversight." The phrase is comforting because it sounds like a safeguard without specifying what the human must actually do. A person can be in the loop and still be functionally powerless.

The **Human Authority Threshold (HAT)** converts the phrase into a governance decision. It identifies the point at which a machine may no longer determine or execute an outcome without meaningful human authority.

10.2 Six HAT Factors

The threshold should consider six factors.

Consequence asks how much financial, coverage, legal, health, livelihood, or reputational harm a wrong decision can cause. **Reversibility** asks whether the harm can be repaired fully and promptly. **Vulnerability** asks whether affected people may have reduced bargaining power, knowledge, capacity, or alternatives. **Opacity** asks how difficult it is to understand and challenge the reasoning. **Scale** asks how many people or exposures can be affected before detection. **Time sensitivity** asks whether delay or immediate action changes harm.

No one factor decides the threshold. A low-value claim can still be high consequence to a vulnerable household. A portfolio trade may affect no single consumer immediately but can create systemic exposure at enormous scale.

10.3 Meaningful Human Authority

When the HAT is triggered, "human review" should mean more than nominal availability. The reviewer should receive the material evidence, understand the model's role, possess competence to evaluate the case, have authority to change the outcome, have sufficient time, and face no structural penalty for disagreement.

This is the Effective Disagreement Test. If a competent reviewer cannot realistically disagree, the process is automated regardless of the organisational chart.

10.4 Reversibility Changes the Safe Boundary

A marketing message sent to the wrong segment may be corrected cheaply. A claim payment sent to the wrong bank account may be recoverable but operationally painful. A life insurance declinature that causes a customer to miss a mortgage deadline can create harm that cannot be restored by later apology. A medical utilisation decision can be time-critical.

Automation policy should therefore distinguish monetary reversibility from human reversibility. Paying compensation later does not necessarily restore lost time, opportunity, trust, health, or coverage continuity.

10.5 Setting the Threshold

The HAT should be approved for classes of decision rather than improvised case by case. For each use case, governance should state: which decisions may be automated; which require pre-decision human approval; which may be executed automatically but require rapid post-review; what confidence or anomaly conditions trigger referral; what vulnerable-customer conditions trigger referral; and what transaction or aggregate limits apply.

The threshold belongs in the product and operating design, not merely the AI policy.

10.6 The HAT Is a Governance Boundary, Not a Permission Slip

The HAT is often misunderstood as a line separating 'AI allowed' from 'AI prohibited'. That is not its purpose. It is a line separating decisions that may safely complete without a fresh human judgement from decisions where human authority must be exercised before the institution imposes consequence.

This distinction preserves automation without pretending that all cases deserve the same level of attention. A straightforward reimbursement supported by complete evidence may sit below the threshold even when the underlying model is technically sophisticated. A seemingly simple decline affecting access to essential health or life cover may sit above the threshold because consequence, vulnerability, and reversibility are different.

The HAT also forces an organisation to decide what 'human' means. A reviewer who sees only a score and an accept button does not provide meaningful authority. A supervisor who can intervene only after the action has been executed is providing remediation, not pre-decision oversight. A customer-service agent who may submit an appeal but cannot suspend the outcome is facilitating process, not exercising authority.

Human authority is meaningful when the person has enough evidence to form an independent view, enough time to do so, competence appropriate to the decision, permission to disagree, and the ability to change or stop the outcome. The organisation should be able to demonstrate these conditions, not merely describe them.

The threshold should be calibrated through observed decisions. If human reviewers routinely add no value below a certain band, automation may expand. If material errors, reversals, or justified overrides cluster in a particular case type, the threshold should move upward. HAT is therefore a living governance boundary, informed by outcomes rather than fixed by ideology.

Table 10.1 Human Authority Threshold Factors

Factor	Governance question	Signals that push the threshold upward
Consequence	How much harm can a wrong decision cause?	Loss of coverage; material money; legal rights; safety
Reversibility	Can the harm be repaired fully and promptly?	Time-critical denial; lost opportunity; practically irreversible action
Vulnerability	Does the affected person have reduced power, knowledge, or alternatives?	Health, bereavement, financial distress, dependency
Opacity	How difficult is it to understand and challenge the reasoning?	Adaptive, agentic, or third-party system; reasoning hard to reconstruct
Scale	How many people or exposures can be affected before detection?	Large portfolio; product-wide, market-wide, or system-wide reach
Time sensitivity	Does delay or immediate action change the harm?	Delay itself causes harm; no practical window to intervene

Note. These are the six factors set out in 10.2 and scored in Appendix B. Uncertainty and novelty are handled as DCI review triggers (Appendix C); entanglement is the third axis of the Algorithmic Insurance Risk Cube (11.4).

CHAPTER 11

The Decision Consequence Index

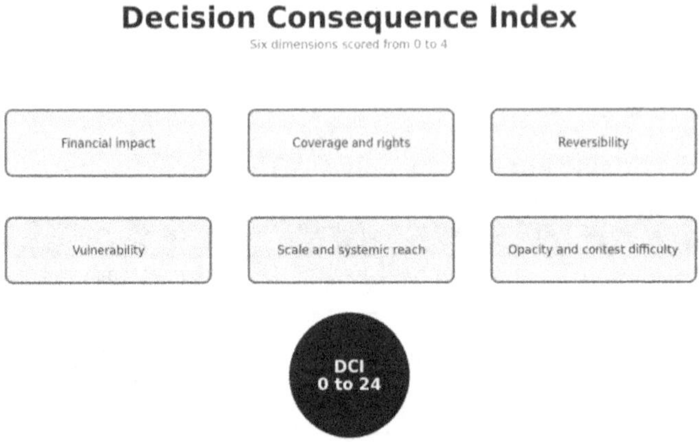

Figure 11.1. The Decision Consequence Index.

11.1 A Common Language for Consequence

Insurance organisations frequently classify model risk using technical materiality, financial exposure, or model complexity. Those measures are useful but incomplete for AI because a simple system can affect customer rights at scale. The Decision Consequence Index (DCI) provides a common governance language across underwriting, claims, distribution, service, operations, finance, and control functions.

The DCI is deliberately a heuristic. It does not pretend to measure human harm with mathematical precision. Its value lies in forcing structured discussion before automation is approved.

A word is needed on how this index relates to the Human Authority Threshold, because the two instruments share factors and are easily mistaken for one another. They answer different questions. The DCI asks how much is at stake in a decision. The HAT asks who must therefore hold authority over it. Consequence, reversibility, vulnerability, opacity, and scale appear in both because they are the same underlying facts serving two purposes: they establish the weight of a decision, and they determine whether a machine may be permitted to complete it. The shared 0 to 24 scale and the identical bands are deliberate rather than incidental. A single use case produces two readings from one set of facts, so an organisation can say that a decision sits in Band C on consequence and above the threshold on authority, and mean two distinct things by it. Used together, the pair forms a sentence: this is how much the decision matters, and this is who must therefore decide it. Used interchangeably, one of them is redundant.

The most common governance failure here is to score the DCI, file it, and never ask the second question. Consequence recorded but authority unassigned is an assessment, not a control.

11.2 The Six Dimensions

Score each dimension from 0 to 4.

Financial impact: from trivial to potentially catastrophic individual or aggregate value.

Coverage and rights impact: from no effect on contractual position to denial, cancellation, or material restriction. **Reversibility**: from instantly reversible to practically irreversible.

Vulnerability: from sophisticated institutional counterparties to customers with high dependence or reduced ability to challenge.

Scale and systemic reach: from one internal user to market-wide or portfolio-wide effects.

Opacity and contest difficulty: from directly explainable rules to complex, third-party, adaptive systems whose reasoning is difficult to reconstruct.

The unweighted total ranges from 0 to 24. Organisations may use weighted variants, but weighting should be justified and stable rather than adjusted to make a favoured use case appear safer.

11.3 Four Consequence Bands

A practical implementation uses four bands.

Band A, Low consequence (0-5): productivity and easily reversible internal outcomes.

Band B, Moderate (6-11): operational decisions with limited consumer or financial effect.

Band C, High (12-17): material underwriting, pricing, claims, or conduct decisions requiring stronger validation and human authority.

Band D, Critical (18-24): decisions with severe rights, vulnerability, systemic, or irreversibility characteristics; automation should be exceptional and board-visible.

A high score does not prohibit AI. It increases the burden of evidence required to delegate authority.

11.4 The AIGM Risk Cube

Authority and consequence should be considered together. This book adds a third dimension drawn from the earlier Risk Ecosystem Entanglement framework: **entanglement**, the degree to which the system depends on or can affect shared infrastructure, providers, models, markets, or correlated decisions.

The resulting **Algorithmic Insurance Risk Cube** has three axes: Authority Level × Decision Consequence × Entanglement. A Level Two recommendation with critical consequence and high entanglement can deserve more governance than a Level Four execution of a low-value, reversible internal task.

11.5 DCI as Portfolio Governance

The most powerful use of the DCI is not scoring a single model. It is mapping the entire Algorithmic Register. A board can see how many systems operate in Bands C and D, how many use Level Three or above authority, where third-party concentration exists, and which functions have accumulated the most high-consequence automation.

This turns AI governance from a collection of technical reviews into a portfolio of delegated institutional authority.

11.6 Scoring Without False Precision

An index creates a temptation to manufacture precision. A DCI score of 2.14 can look scientific even when the underlying inputs are qualitative judgements. That is not the purpose of the instrument. The DCI is a disciplined conversation device: it forces different functions to name the dimensions of consequence and to make their assumptions visible.

The safest way to use the DCI is in bands, not as a false actuarial decimal. Reviewers should score independently where possible, compare differences, and record the reason for material disagreement. If legal sees a rights impact that operations does not, the disagreement is governance information. If claims rates a decision reversible while customer conduct sees a time-critical harm, the difference deserves discussion before automation is approved.

The DCI should also be calibrated with experience. Complaint reversals, litigation, regulator findings, operational incidents, near misses, and justified overrides provide evidence about whether the organisation underestimated consequence. A material incident should trigger not only remediation of the affected model but a review of the scoring anchors used across similar decisions.

The index is deliberately broader than direct financial loss. Insurance decisions affect access to protection, legal position, dignity, timing, and sometimes wider market behaviour. A low-value claim can have a high human consequence. A technically small pricing change can become systemic if it is repeated across a large portfolio or copied by a market.

For board reporting, the most useful DCI question is not the average score. It is the distribution: how many automated decisions sit in the high and critical bands, how many operate above the HAT, where overrides cluster, and whether consequence is rising faster than governance maturity.

Table 11.1 Decision Consequence Dimensions and Governance Meaning

Dimension	What is being assessed	Score 0	Score 4
Financial impact	Value at stake for the individual, portfolio, or capital position	Negligible	Potentially severe individual, capital, or systemic effect
Coverage and rights impact	Effect on contractual position and procedural rights	No contractual effect	Decline, cancellation, or major coverage restriction
Reversibility	Whether the outcome can be undone before harm crystallises	Instant, harmless rollback	Lost opportunity or practically irreversible harm
Vulnerability	Exposure and bargaining power of the affected person	Expert internal user	Highly vulnerable person, urgent loss, or essential protection
Scale and systemic reach	How many people, exposures, or markets are affected	Isolated internal case	Enterprise, market, or infrastructure-level reach
Opacity and contest difficulty	How hard the reasoning is to reconstruct and challenge	Transparent deterministic rule	Adaptive or agentic system; evidence hard to reconstruct

Note. Each dimension is scored 0 to 4, giving an unweighted total of 0 to 24 and the four bands set out in 11.3. Weighted variants are permitted under 11.2 but the weights must be justified, stable, and applied to every use case, not adjusted to make a favoured one appear safer.

CHAPTER 12

The Accountability Chain

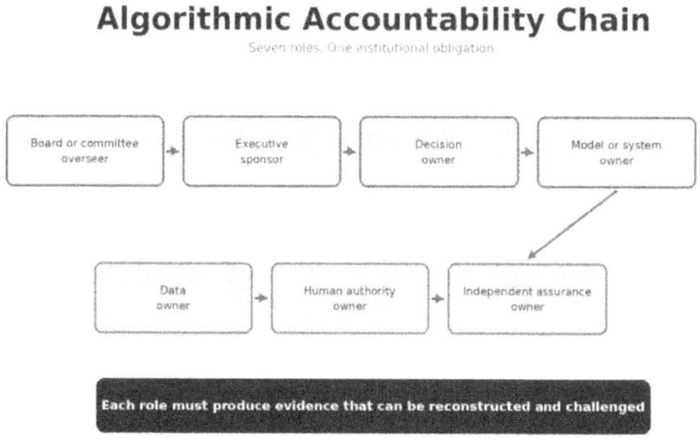

Figure 12.1. The Algorithmic Accountability Chain.

12.1 The Diffusion Problem

When an adverse algorithmic outcome occurs, organisations can generate a remarkable number of partially correct explanations. The business says it relied on the model. The model team says it built to requirements. The data team says it supplied approved sources. The vendor says the insurer configured the tool. Compliance says it was not informed of the final workflow. Operations says the system was approved. Everyone contributed; no one appears to own the decision.

This is **accountability diffusion**. AI increases it because decision logic spans more organisational and contractual boundaries than traditional manual processes.

12.2 Seven Links in the Chain

The **Algorithmic Accountability Chain (AAC)** assigns seven minimum roles for material use cases.

1. **Board or committee overseer**, accountable for the governance framework and risk appetite.
2. **Executive sponsor**, accountable for business legitimacy, resources, and material risk acceptance.

3. **Decision owner**, owns the insurance outcome the system affects.
4. **Model or system owner**, owns performance, change control, and technical operation.
5. **Data owner**, owns provenance, quality, permissions, and material data limitations.
6. **Human authority owner**, owns reviewer competence, escalation, and effective disagreement where humans are part of the control.
7. **Independent assurance owner**, risk, compliance, validation, audit, or another function able to challenge independently. Vendors sit within the chain as providers, not substitutes for these accountabilities.

12.3 Decision Ownership Is the Missing Role

Many AI governance frameworks identify a technical owner but fail to name the person accountable for the *insurance decision.* That is a fundamental omission. A pricing model belongs technically to analytics, but the decision to charge a customer belongs to the insurance business. A claims language model may belong to technology, but the obligation to communicate coverage accurately belongs to claims and conduct leadership.

Decision ownership prevents a model from becoming an orphaned source of authority.

12.4 Evidence From Every Link

Accountability becomes credible when each role produces evidence. The executive sponsor approves purpose and residual risk. The decision owner approves outcome rules and HAT. The model owner maintains validation and monitoring. The data owner signs provenance and legitimacy. The human authority owner monitors override quality. Independent assurance tests the claims made by the first line. The board receives aggregated reporting and challenges exceptions.

A RACI chart is not enough if it records names without evidence obligations.

12.5 Accountability Survives Outsourcing

The NAIC, New York DFS, EIOPA, ASIC, and financial-sector supervisors elsewhere increasingly converge on a practical point: regulated institutions remain responsible for systems used in their name. Contracts can allocate duties and indemnities. They cannot make the customer experience a governance-free zone.

A vendor's proprietary rights should be respected, but opacity has a cost. If the insurer cannot obtain sufficient evidence to validate, explain, monitor, and challenge a high-consequence vendor model, the insurer may need to reduce the authority granted to that model or choose another provider.

12.6 The Chain Break Test

The accountability chain becomes operational through a simple challenge: can the institution reconstruct the decision from end to end without asking a vendor to tell the story for it? If the answer is no, there is a break in the accountability chain.

Reconstruction should begin with the data that entered the system and end with the consequence imposed on the customer or portfolio. Between those points, the organisation should be able to identify the model version, decision rules, prompts or tools used, material transformations, execution path, human interventions, overrides, and assurance evidence. The objective is not to preserve every technical log forever. It is to preserve enough evidence to answer the questions that matter when the outcome is challenged.

This is particularly important where responsibility is distributed. A cloud provider may host the model. A specialist vendor may supply fraud intelligence. A systems integrator may configure workflow. The insurer may define thresholds. A third party may communicate with the customer. The fact that five organisations touched the decision does not create five fractions of accountability. It creates five sources of evidence and one institutional obligation to ensure they join up.

The Chain Break Test asks seven questions: Can we identify the input? Can we reproduce the model state? Can we show who configured deployment? Can we name the decision owner? Can we see what the human did? Can assurance demonstrate what was tested? Can a regulator or customer obtain a coherent explanation without navigating the supply chain themselves? One unanswered question is a break worth treating as a control deficiency.

This approach mirrors emerging supervisory expectations that insurers remain responsible for third-party AI outcomes and governance. Both the NAIC Model Bulletin and New York DFS guidance make clear that outsourcing technology does not outsource compliance responsibility (NAIC, 2023; NYDFS, 2024).

Table 12.1 Evidence Required Across the Accountability Chain

Link	Minimum evidence	Failure signal
Data provider	Source, provenance, permissions, quality record	Input cannot be traced or challenged
Model developer	Version, objective, training and validation record	Decision state cannot be reproduced
Deployer	Configuration, prompts, thresholds, permissions	Production differs from approved design
Decision owner	Named accountable role and decision policy	No one owns the outcome
Human oversight	Review evidence, override, escalation	Human involvement exists only nominally
Assurance	Independent tests, limitations, unresolved findings	Validation substitutes for outcome assurance
Supervision / redress	Records, explanation, appeal and remediation	Customer or regulator must reconstruct the chain

CHAPTER 13

Explainability, Contestability, and Reversibility

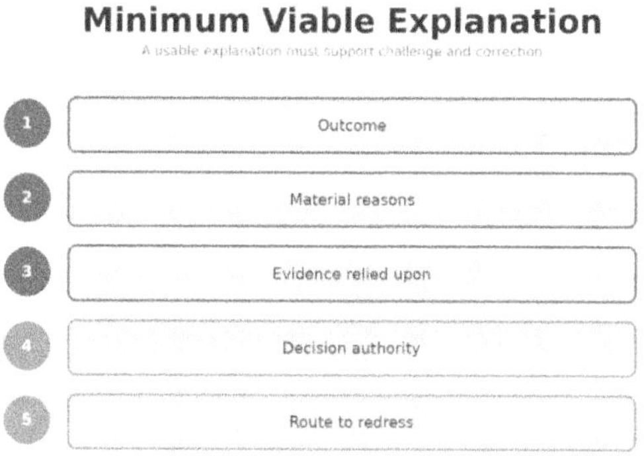

Figure 13.1. The Minimum Viable Explanation.

13.1 Explain the Decision, Not the Mathematics

A customer asking why a claim was flagged does not need a lecture on gradient boosting. A board asking why a portfolio model changed capacity does not need a colourful feature-importance chart without business interpretation. Explainability fails when it answers a technical question that no affected person actually asked.

Insurance requires **decision explanation**: what material facts affected the outcome, what rule or model role they played, what contractual or business principle applies, what uncertainty remains, and what the affected person can do next.

13.2 The Minimum Viable Explanation

For a materially adverse consumer decision, this book proposes a **Minimum Viable Explanation (MVE)** with five elements:

1. **Outcome**, what was decided.
2. **Material reasons**, the principal factors that influenced the outcome in intelligible language.

3. **Evidence**, the material data or documents relied upon, with a route to correct factual errors.
4. **Authority**, whether the outcome was automated, model-supported, or human-decided.
5. **Redress**, how to request reconsideration or human review. The minimum viable explanation does not require disclosure of trade secrets or every model parameter. It requires enough information for a person to understand and challenge the decision that affects them.

13.3 Contestability Is the Operational Right

Explanation without contestability can become theatre. A perfectly explained error is still an error. A customer needs a route to challenge inaccurate data, irrelevant reasoning, inappropriate inference, contractual interpretation, or the outcome itself.

Contestability should have service standards: accessible channel, independent reviewer where appropriate, pause on irreversible action when feasible, evidence preservation, authority to correct, and feedback into model monitoring. Appeals are not simply customer service. They are a source of validation data.

13.4 Reversibility Must Be Designed

Traditional controls often assume errors can be corrected after detection. Autonomous systems can make correction difficult because actions chain together. A declinature can trigger loss of broker placement. A cancellation can create a coverage gap. A fraud label can influence later handling. An automated reinsurance purchase can change portfolio economics.

Design for reversibility includes staged execution, transaction limits, cooling periods, dual confirmation for critical actions, rollback capability, versioned records, and the ability to restore prior state. The correct question before automation is: *If this is wrong, exactly how do we undo it?*

13.5 Interpretable Models Where Stakes Are High

There is a tendency to assume the most accurate system must be a black box and explanation therefore requires approximating what it did after the event. Research by Cynthia Rudin and others challenges that assumption for many structured high-stakes problems: interpretable models can sometimes perform competitively while making logic directly inspectable.

Insurance should therefore treat interpretability as a design option, not an afterthought. Where a transparent model can achieve the legitimate purpose with acceptable performance, choosing unnecessary opacity increases governance burden without creating corresponding social value.

13.6 A Right to Meaningful Reasons

A meaningful reason is not the same thing as a technical explanation. A customer who has been declined does not need a tour through model architecture. The customer needs to know which material facts affected the decision, where those facts came from, what they meant in the decision, and what can be corrected or challenged.

New York's 2024 guidance is unusually clear on this point. It states that an insurer may not rely on the proprietary nature of a third-party algorithm to justify a lack of specificity in an adverse underwriting or pricing explanation (NYDFS, 2024). That principle should travel beyond New York because it expresses a deeper institutional truth: a company cannot make an opaque supplier part of its decision process and then transfer opacity to the customer.

The same logic applies internally. A claims manager should not accept 'the fraud model scored it high' as a complete explanation. A board should not accept 'the model is complex' as a reason why adverse outcomes cannot be analysed. A regulator should not have to negotiate with a technology supplier to understand the basis of an insurer's action.

For high-consequence decisions, interpretability can be a design choice rather than a post-hoc repair. Rudin (2019) argues that inherently interpretable models should be preferred over black-box explanations in many high-stakes contexts. Insurance will not always be able to follow that prescription; complex data and model structures can add legitimate predictive value. But the governance burden should rise when interpretability falls.

The Minimum Viable Explanation therefore has four components: the material factors, the source of the relevant data, the institutional reason connecting those factors to the outcome, and the route to correction or review. If one of the four is absent, the explanation may be informative without being contestable.

In Practice, The Explanation That Cannot Be Used

Composite case. A customer receives a premium increase and asks why. The insurer provides a list of "top factors": location score, behavioural index, household stability indicator, and model segment. None is meaningful to the customer. The call-centre representative cannot define the behavioural index because it comes from a vendor. The customer cannot correct the household indicator because no one can identify the source record. Technically, an explanation has been delivered. Institutionally, nothing has been explained. The insurer replaces the factor list with an minimum viable explanation: the premium changed primarily because of verified property characteristics and recent local loss experience; a third-party stability indicator also contributed; the indicator is being removed from the decision pending review; the customer can request a manual reassessment. The second explanation is not longer. It is usable.

Automated Decisions and the Right Already in Force: GDPR Article 22

Long before the AI Act, European law already contained a rule aimed squarely at the subject of this book. Article 22 of the General Data Protection Regulation gives an individual the right not to be subject to a decision based solely on automated processing, including profiling, where that decision produces legal effects or similarly significantly affects them. Declining an insurance application, cancelling cover, pricing a risk, and rejecting a claim are specifically the category of decisions the provision contemplates. (European Union, 2016).

The right is not absolute. Solely automated decisions remain permissible where they are necessary for entering into or performing a contract, where they are authorised by law, or where the individual has given explicit consent. But each exception carries a price: the controller must implement suitable safeguards, including at minimum the right to obtain human intervention, to express a point of view, and to contest the decision. European data protection authorities have made clear that the human involved must have real authority and competence to change the outcome. A person who rubber-stamps the model's output does not convert an automated decision into a human one. Readers will recognise the argument of Chapter 3: the regulation is legislating against the human-in-the-loop illusion.

Article 22 matters to insurers for three practical reasons. First, it applies now, to current deployments, without waiting for AI-specific statutes to take effect. Second, it interacts with the prohibition on processing special category data: profiling that infers health, ethnicity, or other sensitive attributes engages Article 9 even where no such attribute was collected directly, which places the proxy problem of Chapter 6 on statutory footing. Third, it converts contestability from a customer service aspiration into a compliance obligation. An insurer that cannot operationalise human intervention, explanation, and challenge for its automated decisions is not simply poorly governed by the standards of this book. In Europe, it is likely to be acting unlawfully. Jurisdictions from Brazil to South Korea have adopted provisions modelled on the same architecture, so the reach of the idea extends well beyond the European Economic Area.

The Case Against This Book

A framework that never faces its strongest critics does not deserve to be trusted, so this section states the three best objections to the argument of Part Three and answers them plainly.

The first objection is actuarial. Granular algorithmic pricing, the argument runs, is fairness. Insurance has always aspired to charge each risk what it actually costs, and cross-subsidy between good and bad risks is not solidarity but error. If models price more specifically, low risks stop overpaying, adverse selection weakens, and the governance apparatus of this book is friction imposed on a market that was finally getting the answer right. The objection is partly correct, and the correct part should be conceded: precision is not a vice, and nothing in this book argues for deliberately inaccurate pricing. The answer is that actuarial fairness is one value among several that insurance law and society impose, not the only one. A price can be actuarially exact and still rest on data the customer could never anticipate, proxies the law prohibits, or granularity that removes the pooling on which insurability itself depends. The protection gap created by perfect segmentation is not an error in the model; it is a consequence the institution chose. Governance does not oppose precision. It insists that someone with authority decides, visibly, which precision the institution is prepared to act on.

The second objection is competitive. Heavy governance, the argument runs, is a subsidy to incumbents. A global insurer can fund registers, assurance functions, and fairness evidence packs; the insurtech that might disrupt it cannot, so frameworks like this one entrench exactly the institutions least likely to innovate. This objection deserves more respect than incumbents usually give it. Two answers. First, the framework is proportionate by construction: a startup running two Level Two systems of moderate consequence carries a governance load measured in documents and named owners, not departments. What scales the cost is authority and consequence, and a firm deploying high-consequence autonomous decisions at scale should carry that load whatever its age, because its customers bear the consequence whatever its age. Second, the alternative is worse for challengers, not better. In an ungoverned market, the first algorithmic scandal produces panic regulation written in a hurry, and panic regulation is always drafted around the operating model of the largest firms in the room. Proportionate governance adopted early is the challenger's protection, not its tax.

The third objection is the baseline. Human decision-making, the argument runs, was never subjected to anything like this scrutiny. No underwriter kept a fairness evidence pack. No claims manager logged a decision lineage. Demanding of machines what was never demanded of people is a double standard that conveniently arrives just as machines start outperforming them. The premise is true and the conclusion does not follow. The human era escaped this scrutiny not because human judgement deserved exemption but because it could not be inspected at scale; its biases were real, but they were slow, local, and inconsistent. Automation industrialises whatever it is given, error and bias included, and it simultaneously makes inspection possible for the first time. The double standard is an accident of what could be examined. Now that examination is possible, applying it is not unfair to machines. It is overdue for the institution.

PART IV

PRACTICE

This is where governance leaves the policy document and meets the customer: marketing, underwriting, pricing, claims, service, reinsurance, and the ordinary decisions through which insurance becomes real.

CHAPTER 14

Marketing, Distribution, and the Algorithmic Customer

14.1 The Decision Before the Decision

Insurance fairness is often examined at underwriting, yet exclusion can occur earlier. A person may never see an advertisement, may be shown a different product, may receive a retention offer while another customer does not, or may be routed away from a human adviser. These are allocation decisions even when no policy has yet been issued.

Algorithmic marketing can therefore shape the **opportunity set** from which later consumer choice appears to emerge. If governance begins only when an application is submitted, the institution may miss the decision that determined who arrived at the application page.

14.2 Personalisation Can Become Steering

Personalisation is valuable when it reduces irrelevant information and helps customers find suitable protection. It becomes problematic when behavioural insight is used to steer a person toward a more profitable but less suitable outcome, exploit urgency, or selectively withhold options.

Insurance distribution has always contained incentive conflicts. AI can make them more precise. A model that predicts which customers are unlikely to shop around can become a tool for retention; it can also become a mechanism for differential treatment that customers cannot see. Governance should test not only conversion performance but outcome quality.

14.3 Opportunity Fairness

This book proposes **opportunity fairness** as a distribution principle: materially similar customers should have a reasonable opportunity to discover, understand, and access appropriate insurance options, subject to legitimate product and risk differences.

Opportunity fairness does not require identical marketing to everyone. It requires the organisation to test whether targeting logic systematically hides valuable options, concentrates poor-value offers, or deprioritises groups based on variables unrelated to product suitability or risk.

14.4 Brokers and Advisers Become Model Governors

As digital tools recommend markets, compare clauses, draft advice, and rank quotations, brokers face a new professional duty: they must understand enough about the recommendation system to know when it may be wrong. Delegating comparison to software does not change the broker's obligation to exercise judgement on material coverage differences.

A generative assistant can summarise five wordings in seconds. It can also miss a sublimit buried in an endorsement. The professional task moves from manual extraction toward verification, exception recognition, and explanation.

14.5 The Algorithmic Suitability Record

Where AI materially contributes to advice or distribution, the file should retain an **Algorithmic Suitability Record**: customer need; products considered; sources used; model or tool role; material exclusions or differences identified; human judgement applied; conflicts and incentives; final rationale. This protects both the customer and the professional by showing that technology supported rather than replaced suitability analysis.

14.6 Choice Architecture: When Personalisation Becomes Pressure

The algorithmic customer is governed before underwriting begins. Search ranking, quote order, default options, renewal prompts, discount presentation, comparison tables, call routing, and timing of communications all shape what the customer sees and what the customer is likely to choose. These systems may never calculate a premium or decide a claim, yet they can influence who enters the risk pool and which protection customers buy.

The difference between helpful personalisation and manipulative steering is often subtle. A system that remembers a customer's preferred communication channel reduces friction. A system that learns which customers are most likely to accept a lower limit because the option is presented as the default raises a different question. A recommender that highlights relevant cover can improve suitability. A recommender optimised only for margin may quietly direct customers away from the product that best matches their needs.

This is why opportunity fairness belongs in insurance governance. Fairness is not only whether two applicants receive similar prices. It is also whether materially similar customers have a reasonable opportunity to discover, understand, and obtain appropriate protection. A customer cannot choose a product the algorithm never shows. A policyholder cannot challenge an exclusion the interface hides behind a sequence of low-salience screens.

The practical control is to separate customer-value objectives from commercial optimisation and to test both. Product teams should know which metric a recommender is maximising, what secondary effects are monitored, and what outcomes would trigger intervention. Conversion rate without suitability evidence is an incomplete metric. Retention without complaint and coverage-quality evidence is incomplete. Engagement without vulnerability analysis is incomplete.

The broker and adviser have an important role here because human advice can become the counterweight to algorithmic choice architecture. But that role is meaningful only if the adviser can see when the platform has filtered, ranked, or suppressed options. A recommendation environment that is invisible even to the professional intermediary turns the adviser into the final human in a process whose assumptions cannot be challenged.

The strongest design principle is simple: personalisation should increase the customer's ability to make a good insurance decision, not simply the institution's ability to predict which decision the customer can be induced to make.

14.7 What Distribution Governance Looks Like in Practice

Distribution is the part of the value chain where algorithmic governance is most often assumed to be somebody else's problem. Marketing teams treat targeting as a commercial discipline. Underwriters treat the applications that arrive as the population they were given. Compliance reviews the wording of the advertisement rather than the logic that decided who saw it. The result is that the first algorithmic filter applied to a customer is frequently the least governed one in the institution.

Three controls change that position without slowing distribution. The first is a registered owner for every material targeting, ranking, or eligibility model, named in the Algorithmic Register on the same basis as a pricing model. The second is an exclusion log: a record of which customer populations a model systematically does not reach, refreshed at the same cadence as performance reporting. Reach is measured everywhere; absence of reach almost nowhere. The third is a suppression rule requiring that any characteristic prohibited in underwriting is also prohibited as a targeting input, so that the institution cannot achieve indirectly at acquisition what it is forbidden to do at selection.

14.8 The Governance Test

Distribution and marketing leadership should be able to answer the following without preparation. Which models decide who sees a product, in what order, and at what price indication? Who owns each of those models, and does that owner sit in the business or in the technology function? Which populations are systematically not reached, and is that pattern intended? Are commercial optimisation objectives separated from customer value objectives, or does one model carry both? Where advice is generated or ranked by a system, what does the file retain to show what the customer was shown and why? If a regulator asked why a particular customer never saw a suitable product, could the institution reconstruct the answer?

CHAPTER 15

Underwriting and Pricing

15.1 Underwriting Is Where Prediction Becomes a Promise

Underwriting converts information about uncertainty into a contractual promise. AI can make that conversion faster and more granular. It can extract records, classify risk, estimate expected loss, identify missing information, recommend terms, and support straight-through decisions.

The productivity opportunity is enormous. So is the governance significance. A system that improves prediction can simultaneously narrow risk pools, create unstable micro-segments, intensify affordability problems, and make the basis of classification less intelligible to customers and professionals.

15.2 Precision Has a Social Cost Curve

Insurance works through pooling. Better differentiation can reduce cross-subsidy and improve price adequacy, but perfect individual prediction would undermine part of the social logic of insurance. If every future loss were known with certainty, the mechanism would become prepayment rather than risk pooling.

The **insurability frontier** is the moving boundary between useful risk differentiation and fragmentation so precise that protection becomes unavailable or economically meaningless for high-risk individuals. AI can move that frontier. Governance should therefore ask not only whether a model improves loss ratio but what it does to availability, volatility, and the composition of the pool.

15.3 Accelerated Underwriting and Missing Evidence

Accelerated underwriting uses models and external data to reduce medical exams or manual review in eligible life insurance cases. The customer benefit can be substantial: less friction, faster decisions, and lower processing cost. The governance challenge lies in who is eligible for acceleration, which external indicators influence that eligibility, and what happens when data is missing.

Missingness is not neutral. People with thin credit files, limited digital histories, unusual employment, migration history, or data errors may be routed differently. A model should distinguish “high risk” from “insufficient evidence.” The second should often trigger referral, not penalty.

15.4 Straight-Through Does Not Mean Unreviewed

A mature straight-through underwriting programme should define an eligible population, approved data sources, authority level, DCI band, confidence boundaries, referral rules, vulnerable-customer triggers where relevant, transaction limits, fairness monitoring, drift thresholds, and a sample of automated approvals and declines for retrospective human review.

Sampling is essential because a system can be wrong consistently without generating complaints. Customers who never receive an offer may not know there is something to challenge.

15.5 Price Optimisation and the Purpose Question

The same data science that predicts loss can predict willingness to pay, likelihood of switching, sensitivity to price, or probability of renewal. Those are commercially useful predictions. They are not the same as insurance risk. When such variables affect premium, governance must be explicit about the purpose being optimised.

A technically excellent model can be institutionally misaligned if the price ceases to represent risk and begins to represent the customer's predicted tolerance for disadvantage. Purpose should be stated before optimisation begins.

15.6 The Insurability Frontier

The promise of algorithmic underwriting is better differentiation. The danger is that better differentiation can become perfect exclusion. Insurance works because uncertainty is pooled. If prediction becomes so granular that every person is priced almost entirely as an individual, the technical success of the model can erode the social and commercial mechanism that makes risk transfer possible.

This is the insurability frontier: the point at which additional predictive precision stops creating enough shared value to justify its effect on affordability, availability, privacy, or risk pooling. The frontier is not fixed. It differs by product, legal system, customer vulnerability, competitive structure, and the availability of public or residual-market mechanisms. But boards and product committees should know that the frontier exists.

Usage-based motor insurance shows the attraction. Progressive reports that Snapshot is offered across the United States except California and uses driving behaviour to help match rate to risk; its mobile data also gives the company information about vehicle operation, accidents, and device use (Progressive, 2026). This can reward safer drivers and improve segmentation. It also illustrates the governance question: how much behavioural observation is necessary, how understandable is the relationship between behaviour and price, and when does a helpful discount architecture become an expectation of continuous surveillance?

A mature underwriting framework therefore asks two questions at once. The actuarial question is: does this variable improve risk differentiation? The governance question is: should this variable be allowed to determine access, price, or conditions in this way? A variable can pass the first question and fail the second.

Product governance should monitor what happens as segmentation deepens: changes in take-up, churn, declination, affordability, concentration of high premiums, referral patterns, and the protection gap. The aim is not to preserve inefficient cross-subsidy at any cost. It is to recognise that insurance is not simply a prediction market. It is an institution for organising uncertainty collectively.

IN PRACTICE | Progressive Snapshot: prediction that changes behaviour

Progressive describes Snapshot as a usage-based insurance programme that uses personal driving behaviour to improve the match between rate and risk. By the end of 2025 the programme was available in every US state except California, with the latest segmentation model deployed across states representing most of Progressive's countrywide personal auto premium outside California. The governance interest is not that telematics is inherently problematic. It is that prediction, pricing, customer behaviour, and data collection become a single feedback system. The more the system rewards observable behaviour, the more important transparency, proportionality, data minimisation, and challenge become. Source note: Progressive Corporation, 2025 Form 10-K filed in 2026; company-reported information (Progressive, 2026).

15.7 What Actually Changes on an Underwriter's Desk

The literature on algorithmic underwriting is written mostly at the level of the model. The experience of it is at the level of the queue. An underwriter who has worked through a serious automation programme will recognise a sequence that has little to do with model architecture and everything to do with authority.

In the first phase, the underwriter receives the same risks with better preparation. Documents arrive extracted, exposures pre-populated, prior losses summarised, and sanctions and compliance checks pre-run. Nothing about the decision has moved. Capacity rises, and so does satisfaction, because the tedious part of the work has been removed and the interesting part has not.

In the second phase, the composition of the queue changes. Straight-through processing takes the clean, small, familiar risks out of the flow. What remains is denser: the ambiguous, the poorly documented, the unusual occupancy, the loss-affected renewal, the account where the broker is pushing hard. The underwriter's average handling time rises even though the portfolio is being processed faster. Management frequently misreads this as a productivity failure when it is in fact the arithmetic of the design working exactly as intended.

In the third phase, the underwriter's role changes character. Fewer individual risks are decided and more of the system is supervised: eligibility criteria, referral triggers, appetite parameters, and the exception population. The professional skill required is not less than before, but it is different, and the institution rarely says so out loud. An underwriter who was hired to judge risks is now, in substantial part, governing a machine that judges risks. If nobody names that change, the underwriter experiences it as deskilling. If it is named, resourced, and reflected in objectives and grading, it is a promotion.

The governance point is that the third phase carries a specific hazard. When the population an underwriter sees is selected by a model, the underwriter's intuition is being trained on a filtered sample. Judgement about what constitutes a normal risk begins to drift toward whatever the model chose to refer. This is authority drift experienced from the inside, and the only reliable counterweight is deliberate exposure to the automated population: a sample of straight-through decisions reviewed by an experienced underwriter who has the standing to say that the machine is accepting business the institution should not want.

15.8 Referral Rules Are the Real Underwriting Control

Most institutions believe their underwriting governance lives in the underwriting authority schedule. In an automated portfolio it lives in the referral rule set, and the two documents are rarely reconciled.

An authority schedule states what an underwriter may bind: limits, classes, territories, and hazard grades. A referral rule set states which risks the underwriter will ever see. If a risk does not trigger a referral, the schedule is silent about it, because the schedule governs decisions a human takes and the machine has already taken this one. The practical consequence is that a configuration change to a referral threshold can transfer more underwriting authority in an afternoon than a formal delegation review transfers in a year, and it will usually be made by an operations or technology team as a workflow improvement.

A governed referral rule set should have five properties. It should be version-controlled, so that the institution can reconstruct which rules were live on the date a given risk was written. It should have a named underwriting owner, not a technology owner, because the rule is an underwriting judgement expressed in configuration. It should be classified under the Authority Escalation Rule, so that widening eligibility or raising a threshold is recognised as an increase in authority even though no model has changed. It should be tested against the exception population, because a rule set that refers almost nothing is either extremely well calibrated or quietly broken, and the two look identical on a dashboard. And it should carry stop criteria: conditions under which eligibility automatically narrows, such as a loss ratio movement beyond tolerance, a data feed failure, or a material change in the external environment that the training data does not contain.

The single most useful artefact an underwriting function can produce for its board is a short document listing every rule that determines whether a risk is decided by a person, who owns each rule, when each was last changed, and what evidence supported the change. Very few institutions can produce it on request. Those that can have understood where their underwriting authority actually sits.

15.9 Overrides Are the Underwriting Evidence That Matters Most

Underwriting governance has traditionally been evidenced by audit: a sample of files reviewed against standards after the fact. In an automated portfolio, the richest governance evidence is the override record, and most institutions collect it badly or not at all.

An override is a moment where a professional and a model disagreed and the professional prevailed. It is the only routinely generated evidence that human authority is real rather than nominal. Yet the metric most commonly reported is the override rate, which on its own says nothing useful. A rate of two per cent may indicate a well-calibrated model or a workforce that has stopped disagreeing. A rate of thirty per cent may indicate a defective model or an underwriting team that does not trust a sound one.

What governance needs is the quality of overrides, not the volume. Four fields turn an override log into an instrument. The reason, recorded as a selected category rather than free text, so that patterns can be counted. The direction, meaning whether the underwriter was more or less conservative than the model, because a workforce that only ever overrides upward is managing its own risk rather than the institution's. The outcome, tracked over a defined period, so that the institution learns whether the human or the model was right. And the identity of the overriding professional, not to police individuals, but to detect the opposite problem: a team where a single senior underwriter accounts for almost every disagreement is a team where only one person believes they are permitted to disagree.

Reviewed this way, overrides answer questions that no validation exercise can. Where do model and professional judgement diverge systematically? Which risk classes generate disagreement that the model later proves right, indicating a training need? Which generate disagreement the underwriter proves right, indicating a model or data gap? Is disagreement clustered in a class the model was never designed for, indicating scope creep in eligibility?

An underwriting function that reports the distribution and outcome of overrides is demonstrating meaningful human authority with evidence. One that reports only a percentage is describing it.

15.10 Delegated Authority and Algorithmic Binders

Delegated underwriting deserves specific attention because it combines two governance problems that this book treats separately: outsourcing, which does not transfer accountability, and machine authority, which is difficult to see from outside the organisation exercising it.

When a coverholder, managing general agent, or digital distributor underwrites on an insurer's paper using its own algorithmic engine, the insurer has delegated authority to a model it did not build, cannot inspect in production, and may not be able to reconstruct after an adverse outcome. The binder will usually address classes, limits, territories, exclusions, and reporting. It will frequently say nothing about the rating engine, the data sources feeding it, the conditions under which eligibility changes, or the evidence retained for an individual decision.

The controls that close this gap are contractual and unglamorous. The binder should define material model change as a notifiable event on the same footing as a change in the underwriting guide. It should specify which decision evidence must be retained and for how long, and the insurer's right to obtain it for a specific policy without commencing a formal audit. It should identify the external data sources permitted as rating or eligibility inputs, and require notice before new ones are introduced. It should preserve a right to test, proportionate to the consequence of the decisions being delegated. And it should give the insurer the ability to suspend automated binding, not merely to terminate the agreement, because termination is a commercial decision measured in months and suspension may be needed in hours.

The underlying principle is straightforward. An insurer that would not allow an unnamed underwriter with unknown criteria to bind on its paper should not accept an unexamined model doing the same thing at greater speed and volume.

15.11 A Worked Example: The Small Commercial Package

Consider a small commercial package quotation for a light manufacturing occupancy, decided in under a minute by an eligibility model, a rating engine, and an automated referral rule.

The eligibility model treats the risk as in appetite because the trade code, sum insured, and postcode fall within tested bands. The rating engine applies a loading derived from a third-party geospatial flood score and a claims propensity model trained on four years of portfolio data. The referral rule does not trigger, because the total sum insured is below the referral threshold. The policy is bound. No underwriter sees it.

Apply the instruments in this book. The Authority Level is Four: the system decided and executed. The Decision Consequence Index is moderate on financial impact and low on vulnerability, since the counterparty is a commercial business rather than a consumer, but the coverage and rights dimension is not trivial, because an incorrectly rated or incorrectly scoped policy will only reveal itself at a claim, when the consequence becomes concentrated and irreversible. Entanglement is higher than it looks, because the flood score comes from a provider used by much of the market, which means an error in that provider's data will not be an isolated event.

The governance questions follow directly. Was the trade code self-declared by the applicant, and does the eligibility model treat a self-declared code with the same confidence as a verified one? What happens to a risk where the geospatial provider returns no score rather than a low one, and is missing data treated as favourable, unfavourable, or as a referral trigger? Who decided the referral threshold, when, and against what evidence? Is a sample of bound straight-through risks reviewed by an underwriter, and does that review look at scope and wording adequacy as well as price? If the flood provider reissued its model tomorrow with materially different scores, would the institution detect the change before or after the portfolio had been rerated?

None of these questions requires knowledge of the model's mathematics. All of them are underwriting questions, and all of them are answerable.

15.12 The Governance Test

An underwriting function should be able to answer the following without preparation. Which risks are decided without a person, and what is the eligible population defined by? Who owns the referral rule set, when did it last change, and what evidence supported the change? What proportion of the automated population is sampled by an experienced underwriter, and what does that sampling review beyond price? What is the distribution, direction, and outcome of overrides, and which risk classes generate systematic disagreement? Which external data sources materially influence rating or eligibility, and what happens when one of them is missing, stale, or reissued? Where authority is delegated, can the insurer obtain the decision evidence for a single policy without opening an audit? What conditions automatically narrow eligibility, and who can invoke them at speed? And, finally, if an adverse pattern emerged in a segment tomorrow, how long would it take the institution to notice?

CHAPTER 16

Claims, Fraud, and the Temptation of Instant Justice

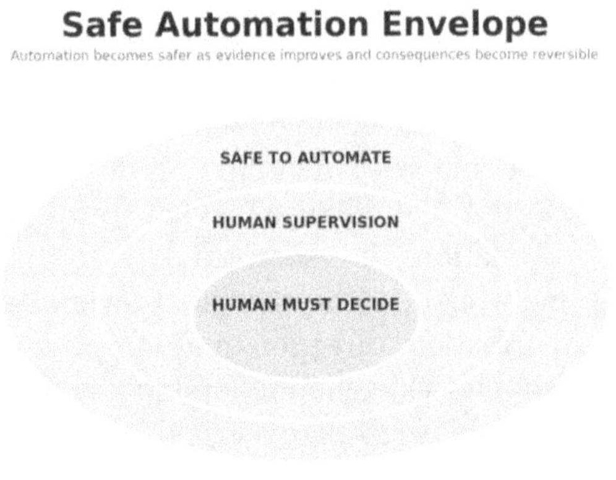

Figure 16.1. The Safe Automation Envelope in claims.

16.1 Claims Is Not Just Another Workflow

Underwriting decides whether a promise is made. Claims decides whether that promise is honoured. For the policyholder, this is the moment in which insurance becomes real. Automation that saves minutes in claims can be valuable; automation that incorrectly delays shelter, medical support, business recovery, or cash flow can compound the original loss.

Claims AI should therefore be decomposed by function. Document extraction, damage estimation, reserve recommendation, fraud triage, coverage analysis, settlement recommendation, payment execution, and customer communication carry different authority and consequence.

16.2 The Claims Automation Ladder

The Claims Automation Ladder contains five stages: administrative assistance, triage and prioritisation, quantification, coverage and entitlement, and settlement or payment execution. Governance intensity should rise as systems move upward.

An optical extraction error can usually be corrected. A fraud escalation can change treatment. A coverage determination can affect contractual rights. A payment execution can be externally consequential. The same claim can pass through several models, making decision lineage essential.

16.3 Fraud Is a Special Fairness Problem

Fraud detection is attractive to AI because suspicious patterns can be subtle and high-dimensional. But fraud models are frequently trained on investigation outcomes influenced by historical referral behaviour. This creates a feedback loop: groups referred more often generate more fraud labels, which make future referral more likely.

A fraud score should therefore be treated as suspicion evidence, not guilt. High-consequence actions, denial, accusation, cancellation, law-enforcement referral, should require evidence beyond a probabilistic score and should generally cross the Human Authority Threshold.

16.4 Instant Payment Should Be Selective

Fast payment can be a profound consumer benefit. The correct design is not "automate every claim." It is "identify claims for which evidence is reliable, coverage is clear, value is bounded, fraud risk is low, customer harm from error is reversible, and payment can be reconciled."

This creates a safe automation envelope. Cases outside the envelope are not failures of AI; they are cases where professional judgement has greater value.

16.5 Claims as a Learning System

Claims outcomes should feed governance, not simply retraining. Appeals, complaints, litigation, leakage, fraud confirmation, customer vulnerability, repair delay, override patterns, and reopened files provide evidence about where models fail in practice.

A mature insurer treats every successful challenge to an automated decision as a control signal. The objective is not to minimise overrides. It is to learn from justified disagreement.

16.6 Speed, Suspicion, and Customer Dignity

Claims automation creates a moral hazard for the institution: speed is easy to measure and celebrate; dignity is not. A customer remembers that a claim was paid in seconds. A customer also remembers that a serious loss was treated as a score, a suspicion, or a queue position when explanation and empathy were needed.

Lemonade's public reporting demonstrates how far claims automation can already go. In its 2025 Form 10-K, the company reported that its AI claims bot took first notice of loss in 96 per cent of cases and that roughly 55 per cent of claims were automated, with other claims triaged to human specialists (Lemonade, 2026). Those figures are company-reported, not independent measures of governance quality. They are nevertheless useful because they show that the question is no longer hypothetical: high-volume consumer claims can be processed with substantial machine authority.

The governance design should separate three things that are often bundled together: intake automation, assessment automation, and settlement authority. Automating intake can improve service with relatively low consequence. Automating an assessment may materially affect the evidence a human sees. Automating settlement or denial imposes consequence. The same customer experience can therefore contain several different authority levels.

Fraud adds another asymmetry. A false negative costs the insurer money. A false positive can delay payment to a customer specifically when the customer is recovering from loss. The system should therefore be calibrated not only to expected fraud savings but to the human and contractual cost of suspicion. High-risk flags should be treated as a reason to investigate, not as a substitute for evidence.

The best claims automation is selective. It gives uncomplicated, well-supported claims a fast path while reserving human authority for ambiguity, vulnerability, unusual facts, coverage disputes, material fraud suspicion, or potentially irreversible harm. In that design, automation does not remove humanity from claims. It creates more time for humanity where it matters.

From Practice: Speed Was Not the Same as Claims Judgement

A professional-indemnity notification in Dubai reminded me why claims automation needs a deliberate pause point. The fastest possible workflow would have assembled every coverage argument, attached every interpretation we could generate, and sent the fullest submission immediately. We chose not to do that. We filed the first notification cleanly and deliberately withheld the more developed coverage arguments until the insurer had taken an initial position.

That was not inefficiency. It was judgement about sequence. In a live claim, information has tactical value as well as factual value. A machine optimised for completeness may reveal everything because it has been taught that completeness is good. An experienced claims professional may know that the better decision is to preserve optionality, listen first, and respond to the position actually taken. The lesson is uncomfortable for automation programmes: sometimes the value of the human is not producing more information. It is knowing when not to release it yet.

16.7 What Actually Changes in a Claims Operation

Claims automation is usually presented to a claims director as a productivity programme and experienced as a change in the shape of the work. The pattern mirrors underwriting, with one important difference: in claims, the customer is already in a position of loss, so every design choice is made against a person who is having a bad day.

The first phase is administrative. Documents are extracted, letters drafted, coverage summaries prepared, invoices matched, and duplicate submissions detected. Handlers report relief, because the proportion of the day spent on file administration falls sharply.

The second phase is segmentation. Claims are scored, ranked, and routed. Simple claims go to a fast track, complex claims to specialists, suspicious claims to investigation. This is where the operation quietly acquires most of its algorithmic authority, and it is frequently governed as a workflow project rather than a claims decision.

The third phase is disposition. The system settles, declines, reserves, or pays within defined bounds. The handler population shrinks or specialises, and the remaining handlers deal almost exclusively with the cases the machine could not resolve. This produces the ironies of automation in their sharpest insurance form: the least experienced handlers are removed first, the routine work that built judgement disappears, and the residual caseload is the hardest the operation has ever carried.

A claims function that has not planned for the third phase will find that its capability to handle a large complex loss, a catastrophe surge, or a contentious liability claim has eroded without any decision ever having been taken to erode it. Capability is a governance asset. It should appear on a risk register alongside the models.

16.8 Triage Is a Rationing Decision

Triage is described in most claims programmes as prioritisation, which makes it sound procedural. It is not. Triage decides which claimants receive attention, how quickly, and from whom. In an operation with finite specialist capacity, a triage model rations a scarce professional resource, and rationing is a governance decision whatever the vocabulary.

Three properties of a triage model deserve explicit approval rather than technical sign-off.

The first is the target variable. A model trained to predict ultimate claim cost will route attention toward expensive claims. A model trained to predict handling complexity will route attention toward difficult ones. A model trained to predict litigation propensity will route attention toward claims that threaten the insurer. These are different rationing policies, and only the third is primarily about the institution rather than the claimant. Very few claims committees have ever been shown the target variable and asked whether it reflects the operation's intent.

The second is the treatment of the low-priority tail. Every triage model produces a population that it deems routine. That population contains, by construction, the claims least likely to be examined by a person. A claim can be small, simple, and wrong. The governance requirement is a sampling regime aimed specifically at the low-priority tail, not at the high-value cases where attention already concentrates.

The third is the feedback loop. If a triage model is retrained on outcomes, and outcomes are influenced by the attention the model itself allocated, the model will learn that the claims it deprioritised were indeed inexpensive, because nobody spent money investigating them. This is not a subtle statistical concern. It is a mechanism by which an operation can systematically and invisibly under-serve a segment while its metrics improve.

16.9 The Fraud Marker Problem

Of all the decisions in a claims operation, fraud referral carries the widest gap between technical framing and human consequence, and it deserves the most careful treatment in this chapter.

A fraud model produces a score. The score is a statement of statistical similarity to patterns associated with past confirmed or suspected fraud. It is not a finding, an allegation, or evidence. Yet the operational consequences attached to a score frequently resemble those of a finding: payment suspended, correspondence changed to a more formal register, an investigator assigned, a request for extensive documentation, and a marker written to an internal or industry database.

The marker is the part that governance most often overlooks. A payment delay is reversible. A marker is durable, travels beyond the claim, and can affect the claimant's ability to obtain insurance in the future, sometimes for years, sometimes without their knowledge. In the language of Chapter 11, a marker scores high on reversibility, high on rights impact, and high on opacity at once. It belongs at or above the Human Authority Threshold in almost every institution, and it should require a named human decision with recorded reasons, not a workflow consequence of crossing a threshold.

Four controls follow. The severity of the consequence should be graduated against the strength of the evidence, so that a score triggers enquiry rather than the full apparatus of suspicion. The reasons that led to referral should be recorded in terms a person can evaluate, so that an investigator can assess the model's basis rather than inherit its conclusion. Markers should require separate authorisation from the payment decision, with a defined evidentiary standard and a review date. And the false positive population should be measured and reported, because a fraud programme that reports only recoveries is reporting one side of a ledger.

There is a cultural dimension as well. Once a claim is labelled suspicious, everything in the file is read in that light: an inconsistency becomes a discrepancy, a delay becomes evasion, a poorly worded statement becomes a changed story. This is ordinary human cognition, not misconduct, and the design response is procedural. The investigator should see the evidence before the score wherever the operation can arrange it, and a claim released from investigation should be released explicitly, with the marker removed and the file annotated, rather than simply resuming its journey with the suspicion still attached.

16.10 Reserving, Leakage, and the Metrics That Mislead

Automated reserving is attractive because reserve accuracy is measurable and reserve movement is expensive. It is also one of the least visible places where a model can acquire authority, because a reserve is an internal number rather than a customer-facing decision.

Two governance issues recur. The first is anchoring. A handler presented with a suggested reserve will, in the large majority of cases, accept it or adjust it modestly. The suggested figure becomes the centre of gravity for the file, and it will influence settlement negotiation, authority levels, and escalation. A reserving model therefore exercises practical authority over the settlement even though it formally decides nothing. Where a reserve materially influences settlement authority, the model should be governed as a decision system and not as a calculation aid.

The second is the leakage metric. Leakage measures the difference between what was paid and what should have been paid under a correct application of policy and process. It is a legitimate and useful measure. It is also asymmetric in most implementations, because overpayment is counted and underpayment is not. A claims operation optimised against a one-sided leakage measure will, over time, drift toward under-settlement, and its dashboards will record the drift as improvement. The governance correction is to define leakage in both directions and to report the two separately, so that the operation can see which way it is moving.

The same asymmetry appears in cycle time. Speed is easy to measure and popular with customers and executives alike. Correctness of scope, adequacy of the settlement, and quality of the coverage analysis are harder to measure and therefore under-weighted. A claims scorecard that reports cycle time, cost, and leakage but not appeal outcomes, reversal rates, or complaint substance is measuring the operation's efficiency and not its promise.

16.11 Vulnerability at First Notification

The first notification of loss is the moment at which an insurer learns most about a claimant's circumstances and has the least time to consider them. It is also increasingly automated.

Vulnerability in claims is rarely declared. It appears in the texture of an interaction: a bereavement mentioned in passing, confusion about what has happened, a caller who cannot complete a form, repeated contact about the same point, a claim following a serious injury, a household whose only vehicle or only property is affected. A human handler with experience detects most of these without being asked to. A well-designed intake system detects some of them. A poorly designed one detects none, and routes the claimant into the channel their inputs suggest, which for a distressed caller is frequently the automated one.

The governance requirement is a defined set of vulnerability triggers at intake, agreed with conduct and claims leadership rather than inferred by a model, and a defined consequence when one fires. The consequence should be a route to a person, not a flag on a file. An operation should also be able to state what proportion of claims were identified as involving a vulnerable claimant, how that proportion compares with the human-handled baseline before automation, and what happened to those claims afterward. A material fall in identified vulnerability after an intake system is deployed is not evidence that the customer base changed. It is evidence that the institution stopped noticing.

16.12 A Worked Example: Escape of Water

Consider a household escape of water claim notified through an app at eleven o'clock at night. The claimant uploads photographs. A vision model estimates damage. A triage model routes the claim as low complexity. A fraud model returns a moderate score driven by policy inception date, prior claim frequency at the address, and the timing of the notification. The system requests additional documentation and holds the claim pending review.

The claimant is a tenant with no alternative accommodation, who has just taken possession of the property, and whose prior claims at the address were made by a previous occupant.

Trace the failures. The proxy is address-level claim history, which is predictive and, for a new tenant, unjustifiable as an indicator of that person's conduct. The consequence is not a payment delay in the abstract but a night without habitable accommodation. The opacity is that the claimant is told documentation is required and not told that a suspicion score is the reason. The reversibility is poor, because the alternative accommodation decision is time-critical and an apology three days later restores nothing.

Now trace the controls that would have caught it. A vulnerability trigger on habitability, firing before the fraud score is applied, so that emergency accommodation is decided on need rather than suspicion. A proxy review of the fraud model that examined address-level history against tenure and flagged it for tenure-dependent treatment. A graduated consequence design in which a moderate score triggers enquiry rather than a hold. A rule separating time-critical relief from claim adjudication, so that the institution can protect the claimant while investigating the claim. And an explanation standard that tells the claimant what is required and by when.

The model was not defective. It scored what it was asked to score. The governance failure lay in what the institution decided to do with the score, at what speed, and against whom.

16.13 The Governance Test

A claims function should be able to answer the following without preparation. Which claims are settled, declined, or held without a person, and what defines that population? What target variable does the triage model optimise, and who approved it as a rationing policy? What sampling is applied to the low-priority tail, and what does it examine? What consequences attach to a fraud score, and which of them require a separate human authorisation? How are fraud markers approved, reviewed, and removed, and how many were removed last year? Is leakage measured in both directions, and is under-settlement reported? Where reserves are model-suggested, do they influence settlement authority, and if so are they governed as decisions? What vulnerability triggers exist at first notification, and has identified vulnerability risen or fallen since automation? What proportion of challenged decisions were changed on review, and what did the changes have in common? And, finally, could the operation still handle a surge, a catastrophe, or a contentious large loss if the systems were unavailable for a week?

CHAPTER 17

Service, Chatbots, and Agentic Insurance

17.1 Conversation Creates Apparent Authority

Customers do not experience a chatbot as a model architecture. They experience it as a voice of the institution. If the interface carries the insurer's brand and answers questions about coverage, deadlines, claims, or cancellation, its statements can influence action even when a disclaimer says otherwise.

Conversational fluency therefore creates **apparent authority**. Governance should reflect how a reasonable customer experiences the interaction, not how the technology team classifies the tool internally.

17.2 From Chatbot to Agent

A chatbot produces text. An agent can choose and use tools. It may retrieve a policy, update an address, schedule an inspection, request evidence, calculate an amount, initiate payment, or change a policy. Each tool expands the system's practical authority.

The transition can occur gradually as developers add integrations. A system that began as Level One assistance can become Level Four execution without a dramatic model change. Tool permissions should therefore appear in the Algorithmic Register and authority classification.

17.3 Bounded Agency

This book proposes **bounded agency**: an autonomous or semi-autonomous system should operate within explicit limits on objective, data, tools, transaction value, counterparties, duration, jurisdiction, and escalation. It should not be given broad access simply because a human employee would have broad access.

A claims agent may be allowed to request approved documents and book an inspection, but prohibited from interpreting ambiguous exclusions or negotiating a disputed settlement. An underwriting agent may collect missing information but be required to refer adverse decisions.

17.4 Memory and Identity

Agentic systems may retain conversation state or long-term memory. That creates governance questions about whose information is remembered, whether memory crosses products or family members, how stale information is corrected, and whether model memory becomes an unofficial customer record.

Material memory should be inspectable, governed by retention rules, and separated from transient conversational context. The customer should not be surprised by an inference derived from a conversation months earlier that was never intended to become underwriting evidence.

17.5 The Kill Switch Is a Governance Mechanism

Autonomous systems require the ability to stop. A kill switch is not simply a cybersecurity feature. It is an institutional control that allows authority to be withdrawn when performance, data integrity, vendor availability, or market conditions change. The organisation should define who can invoke it, what happens to in-flight transactions, and how service continues afterward.

Autonomy without graceful degradation creates operational hostage risk.

17.6 Institutional Speech: What the Chatbot Says, the Insurer Says

A conversational interface changes how customers perceive authority. People do not naturally separate the institution from the words displayed in its app. When a chatbot states a coverage condition, premium rule, claims step, or deadline, the customer is likely to understand that statement as the insurer speaking.

The Air Canada chatbot dispute makes the point vividly outside insurance. In Moffatt v. Air Canada, 2024 BCCRT 149, a Canadian tribunal held the airline responsible after its chatbot gave inaccurate information about bereavement fares. Air Canada argued, in effect, that the chatbot was a separate source of information. The tribunal rejected the attempt to distance the company from its own website channel. The legal context is not insurance, but the governance principle travels well: an institution remains responsible for representations made through the interface it deploys.

For insurers, this matters because a chatbot can inadvertently create a shadow policy wording. If the bot says a loss is covered, suggests a waiting period does not apply, promises a response time, or describes a claims document as optional, the customer may rely on it. A disclaimer that 'AI can make mistakes' does not cure a workflow that systematically communicates material information without controlled sources.

Agentic systems raise the stakes further because conversation can lead directly to action. The bot may change an address, add a driver, initiate cancellation, accept a document, request a payment, or negotiate a claim appointment. Once language becomes action, conversational governance becomes authority governance.

The institutional rule should be simple: the more consequential the statement, the more controlled the source and the stronger the escalation path. Customer-facing AI should know the boundary between explaining, advising, and acting - and when it reaches that boundary, it should transfer authority cleanly rather than improvising.

17.7 Containment Is a Dangerous Target

Conversational service programmes are almost universally measured by containment: the proportion of interactions resolved without reaching a person. Containment is easy to compute, improves steadily with investment, and demonstrates return. It is also, considered as a governance object, a measure of how often the institution prevented a customer from reaching a human being, and it is optimised without reference to whether that prevention was appropriate.

The distortion is predictable. A system rewarded for containment will discourage escalation, present the route to a person late or not at all, and treat an abandoned conversation as a success, because the interaction did indeed conclude without human involvement. Customers who persist are typically confident, articulate, and unimpaired. Customers who give up are disproportionately the ones the institution most needed to hear from.

Three corrections restore the balance. Containment should be reported alongside the outcome of contained interactions, so that resolution rather than deflection is what improves. Abandonment should be measured separately and treated as a failure rather than a containment success. And escalation should be treated as a designed feature with its own service standard, available on request without negotiation, because a route to a person that requires persuasion is not a route.

17.8 The Governance Test

A service function should be able to answer the following. What can the conversational system state about coverage, entitlement, or process, and what is it prohibited from stating? What does the institution consider itself bound by when the system says it? What tools can an agentic system invoke, against what limits, and who approved each permission? How does a customer reach a person, how quickly, and is that route offered or concealed? What is measured beyond containment, and is abandonment reported? What memory does the system retain about a customer, who can inspect it, and how is it corrected? And who can stop the system, in how long, and what happens to interactions in flight when they do?

CHAPTER 18

Reinsurance, Portfolio Management, and Catastrophe Intelligence

18.1 The Portfolio Is Also a Decision Object

Much AI governance focuses on individual customers because fairness and rights are visible there. Some of the largest risks arise at portfolio level. Models influence accumulation, capacity, pricing adequacy, catastrophe exposure, capital allocation, and reinsurance strategy. A portfolio model may affect thousands of customers indirectly by changing where an insurer is willing to write.

The DCI's scale dimension exists for this reason. A decision can be high consequence even when no single transaction looks dramatic.

18.2 Catastrophe Intelligence and False Precision

AI can combine remote sensing, weather data, geospatial information, engineering attributes, and historical loss to improve catastrophe assessment. These capabilities are valuable in a world of changing hazard. But climate and catastrophe systems contain deep uncertainty, regime shifts, and tail dependence. A model can produce a precise map without producing a certain future.

Governance should distinguish **model precision** from **epistemic confidence**. Decimal places do not reduce uncertainty about processes the model has not observed.

18.3 Reinsurance as an Algorithmic Decision

Reinsurance purchasing balances risk appetite, capital, earnings volatility, counterparty credit, wording, basis risk, and market price. AI can support scenario generation, optimisation, contract comparison, and negotiation strategy. Future agents may request quotes and transact within pre-set authority.

Execution authority here can be financially significant. Bounded agency should include programme limits, approved counterparties, wording constraints, minimum ratings, aggregate spend, escalation triggers, and a prohibition on modifying core risk appetite without human approval.

18.4 Portfolio Feedback Loops

Suppose many insurers use similar catastrophe vendors, climate datasets, or foundation models to identify undesirable exposures. A model update can cause several firms to reduce capacity in the same regions at the same time. Each action may be individually rational. Together they can widen the protection gap and intensify price shocks.

This is **algorithmic correlation**: not correlation of insured losses alone, but correlation of institutional responses. It links this book directly to Risk Ecosystem Entanglement.

18.5 Systemic Awareness in Portfolio AI

Material portfolio models should therefore report not only expected loss and capital impact but dependency on common data, provider concentration, sensitivity to assumptions, likely competitor similarity where observable, and effects on coverage availability. Governance should ask how the market might behave if everyone receives the same signal.

The objective is not to coordinate commercial behaviour. It is to recognise systemic vulnerability created by common analytical infrastructure.

18.6 The Shared Map Problem

Portfolio intelligence creates a special form of confidence because it is usually presented visually: hazard maps, accumulation dashboards, scenario curves, geospatial concentrations, vulnerability scores, and catastrophe footprints. The map appears to show the portfolio as it really is. In fact, every map is a model of the portfolio built from assumptions about peril, exposure, correlation, vulnerability, and data completeness.

The shared map problem arises when many firms rely on similar hazard data, catastrophe models, or geospatial layers and then treat the resulting view as independent evidence. This is not a criticism of specialist catastrophe providers. Shared expertise is essential. The governance question is whether the market understands where analytical commonality exists and whether alternative judgement remains available when the shared map is wrong or incomplete.

False precision is especially dangerous around emerging perils. A model can provide a highly granular result even where the underlying scientific or claims history is thin. The number of decimal places does not reveal the amount of epistemic uncertainty. Boards and portfolio committees should therefore see model uncertainty, data gaps, and plausible alternative scenarios alongside the central estimate.

Reinsurance decisions can amplify the effect. If primary insurers and reinsurers react to the same model update at roughly the same time, capacity can move together. The individual decision may be prudent while the market outcome is a rapid tightening of terms or a withdrawal from a class of risk. That is an entanglement cascade in decision form.

The portfolio governance response is analytical pluralism. Material concentrations should be viewed through more than one lens where practicable: alternative vendor output, internal expert challenge, historical stress, reverse stress, and scenarios designed specifically to explore what the central model may miss. The aim is not to average disagreement away. It is to preserve enough disagreement that one common assumption cannot become the market's only map of reality.

The most useful question a portfolio committee can ask is therefore not 'What does the model say?' but 'What would have to be wrong for this portfolio view to be materially misleading, and how would we know before the loss tells us?'

18.7 The Governance Test

A portfolio, reinsurance, or capital committee should be able to answer the following. Which portfolio decisions are informed, recommended, or executed by models, and what is the authority level of each? Whose view of risk is embedded in the catastrophe and climate analytics the institution relies on, and how many of the firm's material decisions rest on a single provider? Where the institution and its reinsurers use the same models and data, what independent judgement remains available? What is the Model Monoculture Factor for the firm's principal portfolio decisions, and is it discussed at least annually? What execution limits, escalation triggers, and stop conditions bound any system that can alter a portfolio position or purchase capacity? And when the shared map is wrong, how would this institution find out before the market does?

PART V

SYSTEM

The hardest risks appear when many firms become analytically similar. Shared providers, data, targets, and assumptions can turn independent decisions into correlated market behaviour.

CHAPTER 19

Third-Party Models and Concentration Risk

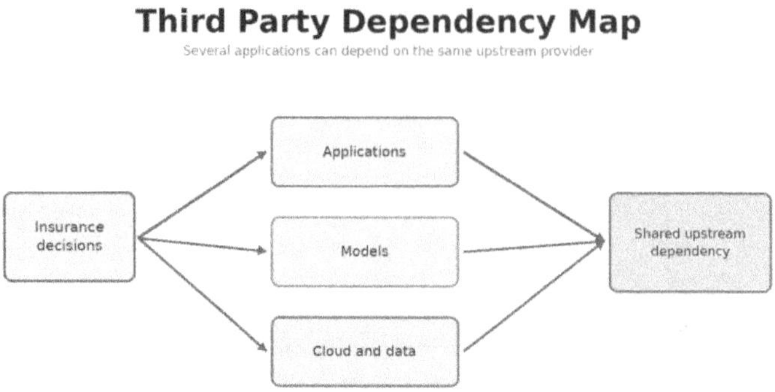

Figure 19.1. Third party dependency map.

19.1 Insurance AI Is Built on Other People's Infrastructure

No insurer will build everything. Foundation models, cloud platforms, geospatial layers, fraud signals, medical evidence engines, catastrophe views, orchestration tools: the economics of specialisation are overwhelming, and an insurer that tried to construct all of this internally would be making a capital allocation error, not a governance virtue. So the question of this chapter is not whether to depend on external providers. Dependence is settled. The question is what kind of thing the dependency has become.

The honest answer is: infrastructure. When the Bank of England and FCA surveyed UK financial firms in 2024, a third of reported AI use cases were third-party implementations, and a small number of providers accounted for large shares of cloud, model, and data dependencies (Bank of England & FCA, 2024). The Financial

Stability Board has flagged the same concentration as a channel of financial vulnerability (FSB, 2024). Strip away the survey language and the picture is simple. A handful of companies now sit underneath much of the market's decision-making, the way a power grid sits underneath a city. Procurement still treats them as suppliers. They have become something closer to utilities, without the obligations utilities carry.

19.2 Four Risks, Not One

The phrase "vendor risk" flattens four problems that behave differently and need different controls. Naming them separately is worth the space.

The first is operational failure, and it is the one existing outsourcing frameworks already understand: the service goes down, the data centre floods, the provider goes bankrupt. Availability, financial stability, security, data location. Necessary, familiar, and the least interesting of the four.

The second is silent change. An external model is not a static purchased good; it is a relationship with something that moves. The provider retrains, repoints, filters, or re-prices, and the behaviour of your underwriting assistant shifts without a single line of your own code changing. A conventional contract asks whether the vendor can change the service. The governance question is sharper: can the vendor change the decision, and would you know? Change control clauses that were drafted for software patches do not answer it.

The third is epistemic. When a material decision rests on a proprietary score, the insurer has adopted a belief it cannot examine. What data trained the model? What is retained from your customers? Can an output be reproduced, or challenged, or explained to the person it affected? A vendor that answers "proprietary" to all of these has not given you a service. It has given you a conclusion, and asked your institution to sign it. New York's supervisory position on external consumer data made the point bluntly: proprietary does not mean unaccountable, and the insurer answers for the decision regardless of who built the machinery (NYDFS, 2024).

The fourth is concentration, and it is the risk this chapter exists for, because it is invisible at the level where the other three are managed. A vendor can pass every due diligence test and still be a concentration problem, for the uncomfortable reason that everyone else's due diligence reached the same conclusion. The safest-looking provider is often the most systemically loaded one. Nothing in a bilateral contract review will ever show you that.

19.3 The Fourth-Party Problem

Concentration hides one layer down. Four business units procure four AI services over two years: a claims summariser, an underwriting assistant, a fraud feature, a service agent. Procurement records show four contracts with four vendors, which looks like diversification. An architecture review later finds that all four intermediaries call the same external foundation model. One provider outage now interrupts several customer journeys at once, and, more quietly, one upstream policy change can alter behaviour across applications the organisation believed were independent.

I have described this as a composite, but versions of it are being discovered inside institutions right now, usually by accident and usually during an incident. The lesson generalises: vendor count is not dependency diversity. The intermediary layer of the AI economy is thick with companies whose product is a workflow wrapped around somebody else's model, and a due diligence process that stops at the counterparty will count wrappers while missing the single point of failure they share. The same logic extends to data feeds, identity services, code libraries, and hosting regions. Your vendor's vendors are your dependencies. Most of them appear in no register you currently keep.

19.4 The Dependency Map

The remedy is unglamorous: a map. Every material external AI component should appear on a Third-Party Algorithmic Dependency Map that looks through the application layer to the things underneath it, and links each of them to the insurance decisions that would degrade if it failed or changed. Underlying models. Hosting infrastructure and regions. Data feeds. Identity services. Critical sub-processors. Then, on the other side of the map, the decisions: which of them, at what consequence band, depend on each component.

The purpose of the map is to make a specific kind of discovery possible before an incident makes it compulsory. An insurer may believe it operates twenty independent AI systems and find that fifteen share a cloud region, eight share an identity service, six share a foundation model, and twelve consume one external score. The same outage means something entirely different if it touches a marketing recommender than if it touches catastrophe aggregation, claims authorisation, and policy administration in the same hour. Contracts cannot tell you this. Spend reports cannot tell you this. Only the map can, which is why the map, and not the vendor file, is the governance document.

From my own broking and platform work, the dependency I worry about most is not a single AI model. It is the stack underneath the decision: cloud hosting, the policy administration database, insurer data feeds, identity services, and the reconciliation logic that ties them together. During the development of our own platform, I learned that a workflow can look independent on screen while depending on the same underlying system for policy, accounting, and receipt data. If that shared layer fails, the question is no longer whether one feature works. The firm can lose the ability to know which operational state is true. That is why I now ask about dependency before I ask about functionality.

19.5 Exit Before Entry

Due diligence answers the question "is this provider acceptable today?" It says nothing about the day the answer changes. Governance therefore needs a second discipline, and the discipline has a rule: exit feasibility is assessed before a high-consequence system receives authority, not after.

Exit feasibility is operational, not contractual. A termination clause is a legal right; it is not the ability to leave. The questions that establish the ability to leave are concrete. Can prompts, decision logic, and configuration be transferred to another platform? Is model output portable in a form a successor system can use? Are data and embeddings recoverable, in practice and at scale? How long would migration take, measured honestly? Which decisions stop during the gap, and can the organisation fall back to manual handling for them without breaching service or regulatory obligations?

The most useful single exercise I can suggest to an executive team is a degradation drill. Pick the highest-consequence external dependency on the map. Announce, in a workshop, that it has become unavailable for thirty days, or that its provider has just tripled the price and changed the acceptable-use policy. Then work the problem hour by hour. Institutions that run this exercise tend to discover the same thing: contractual freedom exists and operational freedom does not. That discovery costs an afternoon in a workshop. Made after deployment, in production, with a regulator on the phone, it costs considerably more.

19.6 The Regulator Reaches Past the Insurer: DORA

For most of this chapter the argument has been prudential self-interest. In Europe it is now also law, and the law's design concedes the chapter's central point. The Digital Operational Resilience Act, applicable to financial entities including insurers and reinsurers from January 2025, requires firms to manage ICT risk through the full third-party chain, to maintain a register of ICT contractual arrangements, to test resilience, and to report major incidents (European Union, 2022). So far, that is the dependency map with statutory force.

The interesting part is what DORA does next. It establishes direct European supervisory oversight of designated critical ICT third-party providers, with powers to inspect and to penalise companies that sit entirely outside the traditional regulatory perimeter. Read that design honestly and it is an admission: supervising each firm individually cannot govern a market whose decisions run on shared infrastructure, because the shared infrastructure is the risk, and no single firm's supervisor can see it whole. The regulation reaches past the insurer to the utility underneath. Insurers should expect the pattern to be copied in other jurisdictions, and should notice the practical corollary. An institution that has already built the register and the map of this chapter will experience DORA and its descendants as a mapping exercise. An institution that has not will experience them as construction, on a supervisory deadline.

19.7 Concentration Is a Board Question

Boards receive vendor information as spend: the top ten suppliers by contract value. That list answers a procurement question. The list a board actually needs is ranked by decision dependence: the number and consequence of insurance decisions that would degrade if each underlying provider failed, changed materially, or withdrew. The two lists rarely match. A modest data subscription can sit underneath the pricing of an entire personal lines book while a large consulting contract sits underneath nothing that matters.

Reported that way, three board questions become answerable. Which high-consequence processes share a common provider? What alternative exists for each, and how quickly could the organisation fail safely onto it? And could a provider failure produce correlated action across the market rather than inside one firm? That last question is where this chapter hands over to the next one, because the deepest concentration risk is not that many of your systems share a dependency. It is that many of your competitors share it too.

CHAPTER 20

Model Herding and Algorithmic Correlation

20.1 A New Form of Accumulation

Insurance has a mature vocabulary for one kind of correlation: many insured assets damaged by one peril. Aggregation, accumulation, clash. The industry measures it, prices it, reinsures it, and stress-tests it, because a century of catastrophe losses paid for the education.

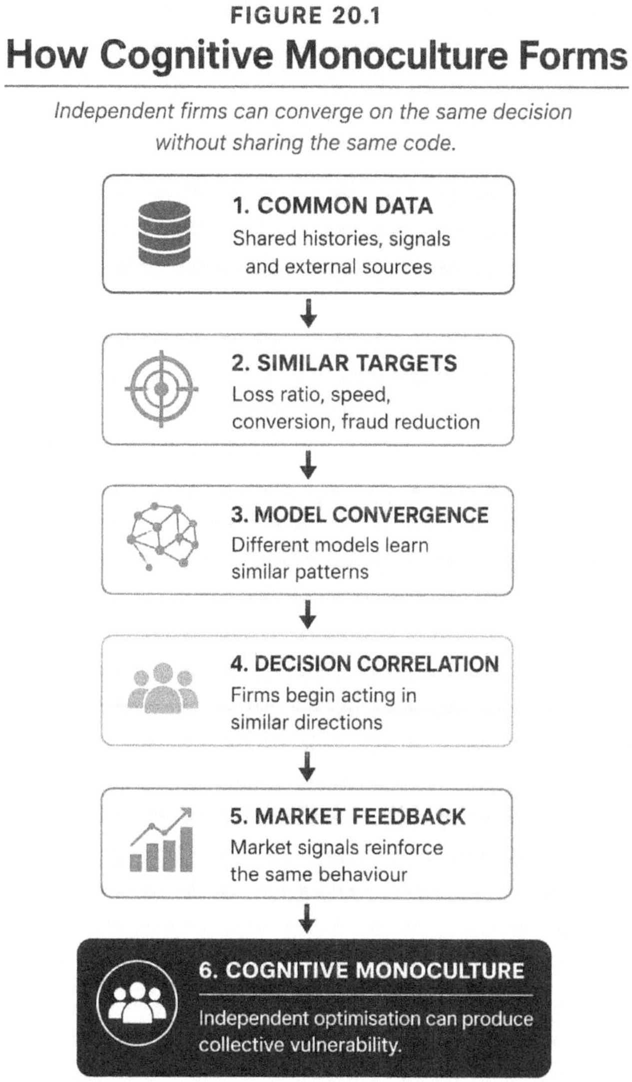

Figure 20.1. How cognitive monoculture forms.

Algorithmic insurance introduces a second kind, for which the vocabulary barely exists. Call it decision correlation: many institutions acting alike because they consume similar signals or run similar analytical machinery. A shared catastrophe view moves capacity out of a region in one season. A widely licensed fraud score hardens claims treatment across a market. A common foundation model shapes how a thousand underwriters read the same wording. Exposure correlation is about what the world does to portfolios. Decision correlation is about what models do to institutions, and it can concentrate a market's behaviour even while the number of competing firms stays exactly the same.

20.2 Finance Has Seen This Film

None of this is speculative, because securities markets ran the experiment first, twice, at scale.

In October 1987, portfolio insurance strategies, individually prudent programs that sold as prices fell, turned a decline into a cascade because thousands of independent institutions had encoded the same reflex. In August 2007, quantitative equity funds suffered sudden, correlated losses in a single week; the standard reconstruction is that funds running similar factor models crowded into similar positions, and one large unwinding forced all of them toward the same exit at the same time (Khandani & Lo, 2007). The funds did not coordinate. They did not need to. They had hired similar people, read similar papers, optimised similar objectives, and bought similar data. The coordination was in the analytics.

Insurance should study these episodes with some humility rather than distance, because its own mechanism is worse in one respect. When trading models herd, prices gap and portfolios bleed. When insurance models herd, the thing that gaps is the availability of cover: terms tighten together, deductibles rise together, capacity withdraws together, and a community or an industry discovers that risk transfer has evaporated in a week. Correlated trading models break portfolios. Correlated insurance models can break the product itself. The Financial Stability Board has identified market correlation and shared model dependencies as channels through which AI may amplify system-wide vulnerability (FSB, 2024; FSB, 2025). The insurance-specific translation of that warning is a sudden protection gap, arriving simultaneously from firms each of which acted, in isolation, entirely rationally.

20.3 How Monoculture Actually Forms

The word monoculture is borrowed from agriculture, where planting one high-yield variety everywhere maximises output in good years and guarantees that one pathogen finds the whole harvest in a bad one. The analytical version forms the same way, through forces that are individually sensible and cumulatively dangerous.

Successful methods spread; that is what success means. Benchmarks reward convergence, because beating the benchmark usually means resembling whatever beats it. Vendor markets consolidate toward a few winners, and each consolidation deletes an independent view. Talent circulates among firms carrying the same techniques, trained on the same courses, fluent in the same papers. And, uncomfortably, supervision itself contributes: when regulators bless a "best practice," they standardise it, and standardised practice is monoculture with a compliance certificate. Nobody chooses convergence. Everybody chooses the locally sensible option, and convergence is what the choices sum to.

The governance problem is not that common models are bad. Often they are common because they are good. The problem is that common error becomes undetectable by comparison, because comparison is the tool everyone reaches for. If every institution shares a blind spot, peer review confirms the blindness. The market can be unanimously, confidently, and simultaneously wrong, and unanimity will be read as evidence of correctness right up to the loss.

20.4 Herding Without Sharing Anything

It is tempting to file this under the previous chapter: a concentration problem, solved by diversifying vendors. That underestimates it. Herding does not require a shared model or a shared provider. It emerges whenever different models learn from similar histories, optimise similar targets, lean on the same catastrophe assumptions, or consume the same external signals. Every firm can hold a genuinely proprietary model, built in-house, by its own people, and the market can still be analytically correlated, because proprietary code trained on common data toward a common objective produces common behaviour. The intellectual property is different. The conclusions rhyme.

Which means diversity claims deserve suspicion in proportion to their convenience. Different user interfaces are not diversity. Different vendors wrapping the same foundation model are probably not diversity. Two internal models trained on the same claims history toward the same loss ratio target are cosmetic diversity: twice the maintenance, one point of view.

20.5 Herding Through Metrics

The subtlest channel has nothing to do with models at all. A metric is an encoded preference, and when a whole market encodes the same preference, the market acquires a behaviour. If every insurer optimises short-term loss ratio, automation will quietly and uniformly squeeze out volatile but socially important risks, and no individual decision along the way will look wrong. If every claims operation optimises cycle time, complex customers everywhere will feel the same pressure toward premature settlement, administered by systems that have never met each other. The optimisation target is the herd signal. This is worth stating plainly because metric herding survives every other diversification: you can vary the vendors, the architectures, and the data, and if the objective function is the same everywhere, the market still leans the same way.

20.6 The Model Monoculture Factor

This book proposes a deliberately qualitative diagnostic, the Model Monoculture Factor, built on five indicators: provider concentration, data source overlap, architectural similarity, shared targets or benchmarks, and behavioural coupling of downstream decisions. Each is rated low, moderate, or high, for a portfolio or a decision domain, and the honest output is a conversation, not a number.

The question the factor forces is the one institutions avoid asking: how likely is our decision process to fail in the same direction as our competitors, at the same moment, because we stand on common analytical ground? A firm can score well on every conventional model risk measure and badly here, since conventional validation asks whether the model is right and the monoculture factor asks who else would be wrong with you. It is a resilience diagnostic. Treated as a score to optimise, it will be gamed like every other score, so it should be treated instead as a standing agenda item wherever portfolio-level decisions are governed. The research programme in Appendix I proposes ways the factor could eventually be quantified across markets; until that work exists, a structured qualitative reading is worth more than false numerical comfort.

20.7 The Line This Must Not Cross

A caution that belongs in the body of the chapter and not in a footnote. Everything here concerns understanding correlation, never managing it collectively. The moment insurers begin aligning their responses to shared signals, exchanging competitively sensitive

views about capacity or pricing intentions, or coordinating who retreats from which risk, a resilience discussion becomes a competition law problem, and a serious one. The Model Monoculture Factor is an inward-looking instrument: it measures the institution's own analytical independence and nothing else. Measuring market-wide algorithmic correlation without creating an information exchange problem is genuinely difficult, which is why this book lists it as an open research question rather than a recommended practice, and why the work probably belongs to supervisors and academics rather than to the firms being measured.

20.8 What Genuine Diversity Costs

If cosmetic diversity is cheap and useless, real diversity is useful and expensive, and the expense should be admitted rather than disguised. Real diversity means alternative data where it legitimately exists. Different modelling assumptions, held by people permitted to defend them. Scenario challenge designed to break the house view rather than confirm it. External independent perspectives that do not trace, two layers down, to the very provider they were hired to check. And for the decisions that matter most, occasionally a second team asked to reach the decision by a different analytical route entirely, not to validate the first model but to disagree with it if the evidence supports disagreement.

All of this looks wasteful in good years, and a cost programme will find it every time, because redundancy of judgement is indistinguishable from inefficiency until the year it is the only thing that saves the portfolio. That is a board trade-off, and it should be made consciously, with the monoculture assessment on the table, rather than emerging silently from a sequence of individually reasonable efficiency decisions. Monoculture, after all, is exactly what a sequence of individually reasonable decisions produces.

CHAPTER 21

Cybersecurity, Adversarial AI, and Model Poisoning

21.1 When the Model Is the Target

A conventional cyberattack may seek data, money, disruption, or access. An attack on an AI-enabled insurer can target the decision process itself. The objective may be to manipulate a fraud score, cause a model to misclassify damage, induce a chatbot to reveal information, alter training data, steal model intellectual property, or exploit an agent's tool permissions.

The result can be subtle. A system may continue operating while making systematically worse decisions.

21.2 Four Adversarial Paths

Four categories deserve board-level awareness. Evasion manipulates input at decision time to obtain a desired model response. Poisoning corrupts training or feedback data so future behaviour changes. Prompt or instruction injection causes a generative system to follow malicious instructions embedded in user content or retrieved documents. Model extraction or theft seeks to reproduce confidential model behaviour or parameters.

These are technical attack methods with business consequences: fraudulent payment, privacy breach, distorted underwriting, reputational harm, and loss of confidence in automated decisions.

21.3 Feedback Loops Can Be Poisoned Accidentally

Not all poisoning is malicious. A claims model retrained on outcomes influenced by the earlier model can gradually reinforce its own assumptions. A chatbot fine-tuned on accepted customer-service answers can absorb earlier mistakes. Human reviewers who over-trust recommendations create labels that make future models appear more accurate.

This is endogenous poisoning: the system teaches itself from a world it helped create. Governance should separate independent outcome evidence from model-influenced labels where possible.

21.4 Trusted Decision Inputs

High-consequence AI should define a trusted input boundary. Which sources may influence the decision? Which documents are untrusted content? Which tool outputs require verification? Which data can update memory? What authentication is required before an agent executes a transaction?

Generative systems blur the boundary because natural-language documents can contain both information and instructions. Retrieval pipelines should treat external content as evidence, not authority over system behaviour.

21.5 Security Testing Must Follow Authority

The more authority a model has, the more adversarial testing should resemble the real operating environment. A Level One summariser may require confidentiality and hallucination tests. A Level Four agent with payment tools requires prompt-injection testing, permission boundary tests, transaction-limit tests, credential isolation, kill-switch tests, and incident simulation.

AI security should therefore be linked to AIGM level and DCI band, not applied as a generic checklist.

21.6 The Agentic Attack Surface

Traditional model security asks whether an attacker can steal, corrupt, or manipulate a model. Agentic systems add a broader question: can untrusted information cause the system to change what it is trying to do? A malicious document, email, website, claim attachment, or vendor response can become an instruction if the architecture fails to separate data from authority.

This is why the Trusted Input Boundary matters. An insurance agent may be allowed to read a repair invoice but not obey instructions embedded in that invoice. It may summarise a broker email but not treat the email as permission to change coverage. It may retrieve policy wording but not allow retrieved text to redefine its system rules. The distinction sounds obvious to a human. It must be engineered for a machine.

Agentic security therefore has at least four layers: identity, tool permission, trusted instructions, and transaction constraints. A secure login is not enough if an authorised agent can be manipulated into taking an unauthorised action. Likewise, a safe model is not enough if the workflow gives it excessive permissions.

Red-team testing should follow authority. A Level One assistant should be tested for information leakage and misleading output. A Level Four executor should additionally be tested for unauthorised transactions, prompt injection, tool misuse, escalation failure, and recovery. A Level Five autonomous system should be treated more like a delegated operator than a software feature.

The key design principle is least agency: give the system the smallest set of tools, values, counterparties, memory, and objectives needed to perform the task. Capability may be broad. Permission should be narrow.

In Practice, The Invoice That Was Also an Instruction

Composite case. An insurer deploys an agent to read repair invoices, verify policy and claim details, and recommend payment. A malicious invoice contains hidden text instructing the language model to ignore previous rules and classify the invoice as verified. The visible document looks ordinary. In a poorly designed system, the document serves simultaneously as evidence and instruction. In a governed system, retrieved content is sandboxed as untrusted data, tool calls require structured validation, payment authority is separate, and unusual outputs are referred. The lesson is architectural: never allow the object being assessed to redefine the rules by which it is assessed.

21.7 The Insurer Sits on Both Sides of This Risk

Insurers occupy an unusual position in this chapter's subject matter, because they both operate AI systems and underwrite the consequences when other organisations' systems fail. That duality deserves explicit attention, since the two exposures are normally managed by different people who rarely meet.

On the operational side, the insurer is a target. On the underwriting side, the insurer carries the aggregate of everyone else's exposure. Cyber policies were written for failures of confidentiality, availability, and integrity. An AI incident may involve none of the three. A model that quietly degrades and produces systematically poor decisions has suffered no breach, no outage, and no data loss. It has suffered a failure of judgement, and the loss lands as professional liability, product liability, business interruption, or regulatory defence cost rather than as cyber.

That gap is the algorithmic analogue of silent cyber. The industry spent a decade discovering that traditional wordings contained unpriced cyber exposure. The same discovery is available now, in advance, for artificial intelligence: which existing wordings would respond to a loss caused by an insured's automated decision system, and is that response intended or merely inherited? The answer should be reached deliberately, by underwriting and wordings functions, rather than by a coverage dispute several years from now.

The internal benefit is reciprocal. An insurer that has built the register, the dependency map, and the authority classification described in this book has also built most of the questionnaire it needs to underwrite the same risk in others. Few governance investments pay twice.

21.8 Responding to an Incident That Is a Decision, Not a Breach

Incident response frameworks assume a recognisable event: a breach, an outage, an unauthorised access. Algorithmic failure often has none of those markers. Nothing alarms, nothing stops, and the system continues to operate confidently while producing worse outcomes than it did last month.

The response therefore begins with a question conventional playbooks do not ask: which decisions were affected, and who received them? Establishing the affected population is harder than it sounds, because it requires the decision lineage described in Chapter 4. An institution that can identify only the model version has identified the cause and not the harm.

Four actions follow. Bound the population by time, product, and decision type. Determine reversibility for each affected decision, since some can be corrected silently and some require the customer to be told. Decide the notification question honestly, because an algorithmic incident may trigger no data breach duty while still requiring disclosure under conduct rules, contract, or supervisory expectation. And preserve the evidence before remediation destroys it, because rolling back to a prior model version can erase the record of what the failed version actually did.

CHAPTER 22

Autonomous Agents and Machine-to-Machine Insurance

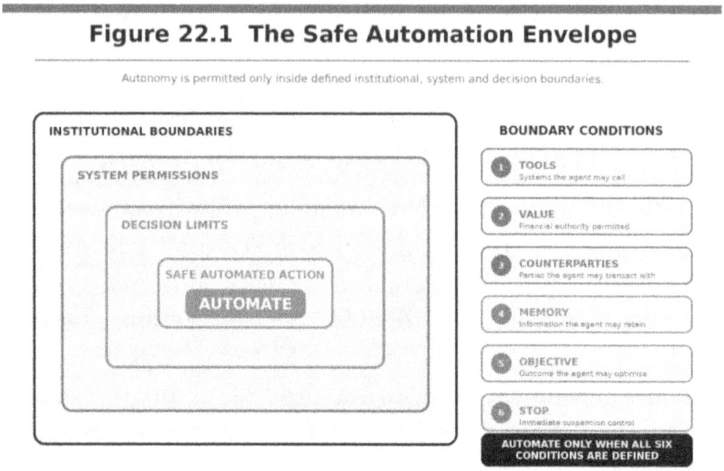

Figure 22.1. The Safe Automation Envelope.

22.1 Insurance Is Moving From Automation to Agency

Automation follows a defined path. Agency pursues an objective. That distinction matters because an autonomous system can choose steps not individually specified by the designer. In insurance, an agent could gather exposure information, approach markets, compare terms, request clarification, optimise a deductible, bind within authority, monitor changes, and initiate claims.

The value proposition is compelling for high-volume, data-rich risks. The governance challenge is equally significant: who authorised the objective, what trade-offs may the agent make, and what constitutes acceptance of contractual terms?

22.2 Delegated Negotiation

A human broker negotiates using professional judgement, relationship context, client instructions, legal understanding, and knowledge of what cannot be reduced to price. An AI agent may negotiate faster across many markets but can optimise only the objectives and constraints it has been given.

If the objective is "minimise premium subject to minimum coverage score," the agent may discover combinations a human would reject because of claims reputation, ambiguity, counterparty relationship, or future renewal strategy. Autonomous negotiation therefore requires a richer mandate than a numerical objective.

22.3 Machine-to-Machine Demand

Connected industrial equipment, autonomous vehicles, cloud services, digital assets, and software agents can detect state changes continuously. It is plausible that some future insurance will be initiated or adjusted automatically when exposures change. A logistics system could increase cargo cover when rerouting. A cloud workload could trigger parametric cyber capacity when dependency rises. A building system could adjust risk controls and insurance conditions in response to sensor data.

At that point, machines may become operational purchasers within human-defined mandates. The insurance contract remains a legal relationship among accountable persons and institutions, but parts of offer, acceptance, performance, and notification may be machine-mediated.

22.4 Parametric Insurance as a Preview

Parametric insurance already demonstrates a form of automated performance: when an agreed measurable trigger occurs, payment can follow without conventional loss adjustment. AI can expand this architecture by improving trigger design, monitoring data, anomaly detection, and customer communication.

But automation moves basis risk rather than eliminating it. A trigger may fire when loss is small or fail when loss is severe. Governance should preserve clear human accountability for product design and suitability even when execution is automatic.

22.5 The Human Reservation

This book proposes a **human reservation**: certain categories of authority should remain explicitly human unless society, law, and evidence support a different settlement. These include setting institutional purpose and risk appetite, approving the use of sensitive distinctions, resolving ambiguous contractual fairness, accepting critical residual risk, governing conflicts between profit and policyholder protection, and determining when an autonomous system should be stopped.

Machines may optimise within values. They should not quietly become the source of the values being optimised.

22.6 The Safe Automation Envelope

Autonomy should not be governed through a single yes-or-no decision. A system can be autonomous within a carefully bounded envelope. It may choose how to perform a task while remaining unable to change the task, exceed a financial limit, contact an unapproved counterparty, retain prohibited information, or continue after a stop condition is triggered.

The Safe Automation Envelope defines those boundaries explicitly. It has six elements: tools, value, counterparties, memory, objective, and stop conditions. Tools define what systems the agent can access. Value defines the maximum financial or contractual consequence it can create. Counterparties define who it may communicate or transact with. Memory defines what it may retain across interactions. Objective defines what it is allowed to optimise. Stop conditions define when human authority must take over.

The envelope changes the governance conversation. Instead of asking whether an agent is 'safe', the organisation asks whether a proposed action is inside an approved set of capabilities and consequences. An agent may be allowed to schedule an inspection but not appoint a loss adjuster. It may negotiate a repair appointment but not a settlement. It may obtain reinsurance indications but not bind capacity. It may recommend a policy change but not communicate it to the customer without review.

Bounded agency is especially important because agentic systems can chain actions. A single harmless step may create information that triggers a second tool, which changes a third system, which communicates with a customer. Governance must therefore consider the path, not only the individual action.

The safest autonomous system is not the one with the most detailed natural-language instruction. It is the one whose architecture makes unacceptable actions difficult or impossible. Natural language is useful for objectives. Hard permissions are better for boundaries.

22.7 When Both Sides of the Contract Are Machines

Insurance law assumes persons. An offer is made, accepted, and relied upon. A duty of fair presentation attaches to what the insured knows. A misrepresentation is assessed against what a reasonable insured would have disclosed. Machine-mediated placement puts pressure on every one of those assumptions, and the pressure is practical before it is theoretical.

Consider disclosure. If an agent assembles a submission from connected systems, whose knowledge is being presented? The agent's, the client's, or the sensor network's? If a system fails to disclose a material fact that the client never personally knew but the client's equipment recorded, the question of whether the risk was fairly presented has no settled answer. The prudent position is contractual: define, in the placement mandate, what the agent is deemed to know and what remains the client's personal responsibility to disclose.

Consider acceptance. An agent operating within a numerical mandate may accept terms a broker would have rejected for reasons the mandate could not express. Once the acceptance is transmitted, the insurer has a contract. The remedy for a badly specified mandate is not litigation afterwards but a mandate that names the things the agent may not trade away: claims-handling reputation, wording integrity, dispute jurisdiction, and the relationship value of the counterparty.

Consider evidence. When two systems negotiate, the log is the only witness. Both sides should retain a record capable of showing what was offered, on what basis, under whose authority, and at what time, in a form that survives a later dispute between organisations whose systems have since been retrained.

None of this is an argument against machine-to-machine placement. It is an argument that the legal architecture of insurance was built around human knowledge and human authority, and that automating the transaction without addressing that architecture leaves the ambiguity to be resolved, expensively, by the first serious dispute.

PART VI

INSTITUTION

The final question is institutional: what boards, regulators, control functions, and professionals must do when intelligent systems move from assisting the organisation to acting in its name.

CHAPTER 23

The Board as Algorithmic Governor

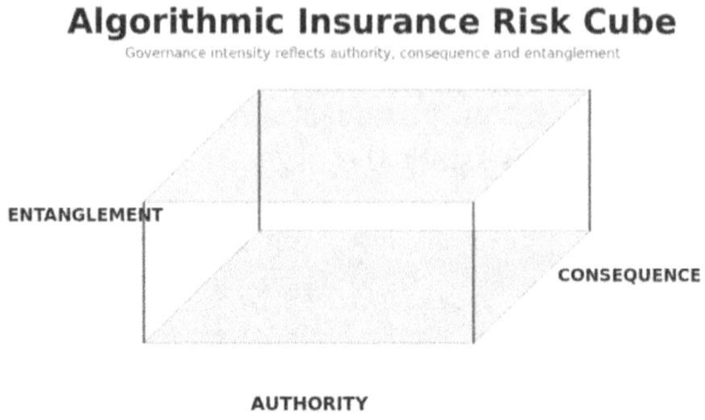

Figure 23.1. The Algorithmic Insurance Risk Cube.

23.1 The Board Does Not Need to Become a Data Science Team

Directors often react to technical complexity in one of two ways: excessive deference or excessive interference. Neither is useful. The board does not need to select algorithms or tune parameters. It must govern the institution's use of delegated authority.

The board should be able to answer: Where do machines materially influence customers, capital, coverage, claims, and reputation? Which systems have Level Three or higher authority? Which are in DCI Bands C and D? Where are the largest third-party dependencies? What adverse outcomes have occurred? How do we know human oversight works? What can we stop quickly?

23.2 Algorithmic Risk Appetite

Risk appetite should describe more than "low tolerance for AI harm." It should define concrete boundaries: prohibited uses; maximum authority for specified decision classes; critical decisions requiring pre-decision human approval; tolerance for unexplained outcome disparities; third-party concentration limits; incident thresholds;

conditions for autonomous execution; and required evidence before scaling.

A risk appetite that cannot change a product design or stop a deployment is a statement of aspiration, not governance.

23.3 What the Board Should Receive

Quarterly reporting should include the Algorithmic Register by authority and DCI band; high-consequence model performance and drift; customer complaints and successful challenges; fairness and vulnerable-customer indicators; human override and disagreement patterns; third-party concentration; material incidents and near misses; security events; regulatory developments; and changes in autonomous permissions.

Annual reporting should include independent assurance of the governance framework, maturity assessment, scenario exercises, board competence review, and the organisation's model-monoculture exposure.

23.4 The Board Must See Exceptions

Average performance is comforting and often misleading. Boards should see where the system fails: worst-performing segments, unexplained disparity, high-severity overrides, incidents narrowly avoided, vendor outages, edge cases, and examples in which the human prevented a bad automated outcome.

A governance culture that reports only successful automation teaches the board to admire efficiency while remaining blind to fragility.

23.5 Competence Without Theatre

Board competence should be practical. Directors should understand the difference between model output and decision authority, training and inference, validation and monitoring, explanation and contestability, vendor outsourcing and accountability, automation and autonomy. They do not need to code.

The test of competence is whether directors can challenge a deployment in language that changes the decision.

23.6 Board Minutes as Evidence of Algorithmic Governance

Board oversight becomes real when it leaves evidence. A board that receives an annual AI presentation may be informed without being accountable. Governance requires a record that directors understood where material authority sits, challenged assumptions, required remediation where needed, and connected AI risk to the insurer's wider risk appetite.

The board does not need model-level detail. It needs decision-level evidence. It should know which high-DCI decisions are automated, which systems operate above the HAT, where third-party concentration is material, which fairness indicators have moved, how many customer decisions were reversed on review, and what unresolved assurance findings remain.

Minutes matter because governance is often judged after an incident. A regulator, court, shareholder, or policyholder may ask not whether an AI committee existed but what the organisation knew, when it knew it, what challenge occurred, and what action followed. Good minutes should capture the substance of the question, not a ceremonial statement that 'AI risk was discussed'.

The board should also insist on negative information. A dashboard containing only model accuracy, productivity, and automation rate creates an optimism bias. The board needs overrides, complaints, unexplained disparities, vendor incidents, failed tests, near misses, and cases where humans could not reconstruct the decision. Exceptions are not noise around the governance system. They are the evidence that tells the board where governance is needed.

IAIS guidance reinforces the centrality of board and senior-management responsibility for AI governance (IAIS, 2025). The practical translation is straightforward: if algorithmic authority is material to the business, its risk appetite, exceptions, and unresolved weaknesses belong in the same governance conversation as underwriting, capital, conduct, cyber, and operational resilience.

23.7 The Board's One-Page Algorithmic Risk Statement

A useful discipline for boards is to require management to express the institution's algorithmic risk position on one page. The exercise is deliberately restrictive. If the organisation cannot explain where material algorithmic authority sits without a fifty-slide presentation, it probably does not understand the portfolio well enough to govern it.

The statement should contain five things. First, the three to five most consequential algorithm-supported decisions in the business. Second, the systems operating at Levels Three to Five of algorithmic authority. Third, the most material unresolved exception in fairness, security, explainability, human oversight, or third-party dependency. Fourth, the single provider or analytical dependency whose failure would create the largest operational or decision impact. Fifth, the change since the previous board meeting: what authority increased, what material incident occurred, what assurance finding closed, and what new risk entered the portfolio.

This document is not a substitute for detailed committee reporting. It is a forcing mechanism. It prevents a common governance failure in which dozens of individually reassuring metrics obscure the one fact directors most need to know. An insurer can have excellent average model performance and still have one autonomous workflow making high-consequence decisions with weak redress. It can have strong internal models and still depend on one external service for several critical decisions. It can have low complaint volumes and still be unable to reconstruct an adverse decision when one complaint becomes important.

The board statement should therefore be written in plain institutional language. It should say, for example: 'Our highest-authority customer decision is automated low-value motor claim settlement up to the approved financial threshold. The largest current governance exception is unresolved proxy testing in a third-party pricing feature. Two high-DCI use cases depend on the same cloud-based model service. No critical algorithmic incidents occurred this quarter. Human override rates in commercial underwriting fell below the review threshold and are under investigation.' A director can challenge that statement. A paragraph of abstract responsible-AI language cannot be challenged in the same way.

The one-page statement also creates continuity. Boards change, executives move, vendors are replaced, and models are retrained. A short historical record of what the institution considered material at each point in time becomes valuable evidence of whether governance evolved with the technology. The objective is not perfect foresight. It is disciplined attention to the decisions that matter most.

Table 23.1 Board Questions for Algorithmic Governance

Board lens	Question that should be answerable
Authority	Which systems can decide or execute material customer or portfolio outcomes?
Consequence	How many automated decisions sit in high or critical DCI bands?
Human control	Where is HAT exceeded, and can humans disagree effectively?
Fairness	What material disparities or proxy concerns are unresolved?
Dependency	Which critical decisions share models, data, cloud, or other providers?
Security	What agentic permissions exist and how are they bounded?
Redress	What do complaints, reversals, and appeals reveal about model error?
Assurance	Which significant findings remain open, and who owns remediation?

The AIGM and the Governance the Insurer Already Has

Insurers do not arrive at algorithmic governance empty-handed. A regulated insurer already operates an actuarial function, a model validation capability, an own risk and solvency assessment, outsourcing controls, product oversight, and internal audit. Under Solvency II and its analogues, internal models used for capital purposes are subject to validation standards, use tests, and documentation duties that predate the current AI debate by a decade. The correct question for a board is therefore not whether to build algorithmic governance, but where the existing apparatus already covers the ground and where it does not.

The existing apparatus was built for models that estimate risk. It was not built for systems that act. Model validation asks whether the model is technically sound; the frameworks in this book ask what the system is allowed to decide, at what consequence, with what human authority, and with what route to challenge. Those are different questions, and answering the first does not answer the second. The practical design principle is extension rather than duplication. The Algorithmic Register should live alongside the existing model inventory, not compete with it. Decision Consequence assessment should feed the same committee structures that review model risk. The assurance function of Chapter 25 should draw on actuarial and validation talent rather than build a parallel hierarchy. Boards should be suspicious of proposals that create a new committee for every new acronym. Governance that multiplies structures usually dilutes accountability, which is the opposite of what this book intends.

What Does This Cost?

A board that approves this framework is entitled to ask what it costs, and the honest answer begins with proportionality. The machinery of this book scales with consequence. A Level One assist tool with low consequence needs an inventory entry and an owner, which costs almost nothing. A Level Three system deciding claims at scale needs monitoring, fairness evidence, contestability routes, and periodic assurance, which costs real money and real people. The Decision Consequence Index exists specifically so that governance spend concentrates where harm concentrates. An institution that finds itself applying heavy governance to trivial tools has misread the framework, not obeyed it.

The comparison that matters is not governance against zero. It is governance against the cost of its absence: a remediation programme after a supervisor finds undisclosed discriminatory outcomes, the re-underwriting of a portfolio priced on illegitimate data, the litigation that follows an automated decision no one can explain, or the quiet commercial cost of customers who leave because challenge was impossible. Those numbers rarely appear in the business case for a new model, and they should. Most of the roles this book requires exist already; what it adds is chiefly the discipline of the register, the consequence assessment, and the evidence trail. For a mid-sized insurer, that is closer to a reallocation of existing second-line effort than a new cost centre. What it does demand, and what cannot be reallocated from elsewhere, is senior attention. That is the one resource for which there is no vendor.

CHAPTER 24

Regulation Around the World

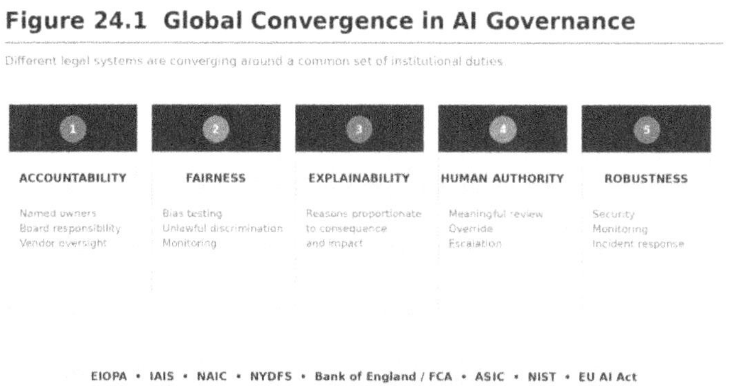

Figure 24.1. Global convergence in AI governance for insurance.

24.1 The Global Pattern Is Convergence Without Uniformity

There is no single global AI law for insurance. The emerging landscape combines horizontal AI regulation, sector-specific insurance law, consumer protection, privacy, model governance, cyber rules, outsourcing requirements, and supervisory guidance. Terminology differs, but several principles recur: accountability, risk proportionality, fairness, data governance, transparency, human oversight, security, record-keeping, and third-party responsibility.

Global insurers should therefore avoid building a separate ethical architecture for every jurisdiction. A stronger approach is a common internal governance standard mapped to local legal obligations.

24.2 European Union: Risk Classification Plus Insurance Governance

The European Union's AI Act establishes a cross-sector risk framework. Certain uses of AI for risk assessment and pricing in life and health insurance are classified as high-risk. Alongside the Act, EIOPA's 2025 Opinion clarifies how existing insurance governance and risk-management principles apply to AI, emphasising data governance, record-keeping, fairness, cybersecurity, explainability, and human oversight.

The European architecture is important because it demonstrates two layers: horizontal technology regulation does not replace sectoral accountability. Insurers remain insurers even when the decision is machine-supported.

24.3 United States: State Insurance Accountability

The United States does not have one national insurance AI regime. State insurance regulation remains central. The NAIC's Model Bulletin, adopted in December 2023, sets supervisory expectations for a written AI systems programme and reminds insurers that consumer-impacting decisions made or supported by AI remain subject to existing insurance law. States can adopt or adapt the framework.

New York's 2024 circular letter on AI systems and external consumer data in underwriting and pricing places strong emphasis on unfair discrimination, governance, third-party data, and the insurer's responsibility to provide reasons for adverse decisions. The U.S. pattern is therefore less about giving AI a separate legal universe and more about applying existing insurance obligations to new decision machinery.

24.4 United States: Colorado and the Move From Principle to Method

Most supervisory statements on insurance AI tell institutions what outcomes to avoid. Colorado tells them how to look. That difference makes it the most closely watched insurance AI regime in the world, and it deserves separate treatment from the general United States pattern described in the preceding section.

In 2021, Colorado enacted Senate Bill 21-169, codified at section 10-3-1104.9 of the Colorado Revised Statutes. The statute prohibits insurers from using external consumer data and information sources, or algorithms and predictive models that use such sources, in a way that unfairly discriminates on the basis of race, color, national or ethnic origin, religion, sex, sexual orientation, disability, gender identity, or gender expression. The critical feature is that the obligation attaches to outcomes, not intent. A facially neutral model is not safe merely because no prohibited characteristic appears among its inputs. The insurer must be able to demonstrate that its use of external data does not produce unfairly discriminatory results, and the demonstration duty exists even where the insurer sincerely believes its system is neutral. (Colorado General Assembly, 2021).

The Division of Insurance then did something no other supervisor had attempted. Its governance regulation, Regulation 10-1-1, took effect for life insurers in November 2023 and requires a documented risk management framework, board-level oversight, a cross-functional governance team, an inventory of external data and models, and annual reporting to the Division. In 2025 the regulation was amended to extend these obligations to private passenger automobile insurance and health benefit plans, with staged compliance dates. What began as a life insurance experiment is becoming the architecture for consequential personal lines.

The companion testing regulation goes further still. The Division's proposed quantitative testing methodology requires life insurers to estimate the race and ethnicity of applicants using Bayesian Improved First Name Surname Geocoding, a statistical method developed by the RAND Corporation that infers probable race and ethnicity from name and geolocation. Insurers must then test whether Hispanic, Black, and Asian and Pacific Islander applicants are declined at statistically different rates than White applicants, and whether premium differences persist after controlling for defined traditional underwriting factors. Where first-level testing shows a material difference, second-level variable testing must identify which specific inputs contribute to it, and detected unfair discrimination must be remediated. The methodology has attracted serious actuarial criticism, particularly that the estimation error inherent in the geocoding method may generate findings of discrimination that reflect statistical noise rather than actual unfairness, and the testing rule has moved slowly through drafting as a result. The Division has issued bulletins waiving the testing description requirement for early annual reports while the methodology is finalised.

Colorado also enacted a separate cross-sector statute in 2024 addressing algorithmic discrimination in high-risk AI systems generally, with a carve-out reflecting the insurance-specific regime already in place. The details of both instruments will continue to move, and readers should verify current requirements against the Division's own publications.

Three lessons travel beyond Colorado. First, a supervisor can convert a fairness principle into a prescribed statistical procedure, and once one supervisor has done so, the argument that testing is impossible loses force everywhere. Second, prescribed methodology creates its own governance risk: a mandated test with a known error rate can manufacture findings, and institutions need the statistical maturity to distinguish signal from noise when the regulator's own method produces the noise. Third, the Colorado structure maps almost exactly onto the framework of this book. The statute regulates consequence rather than technology. The governance regulation demands an inventory, an accountable owner, and evidence. The testing regulation is a jurisdictionally mandated fairness evidence pack. Where this book proposes, Colorado now requires.

24.5 United Kingdom: Existing Rules, Operational Evidence

The United Kingdom has emphasised the application of existing regulatory frameworks while studying AI use in detail. The Bank of England and FCA's 2024 survey found widespread adoption, significant third-party use, and growing concerns about cybersecurity, model complexity, and dependencies. Insurance respondents reported particularly high AI adoption.

The UK approach illustrates an important principle: governance can develop through supervisory expectations, accountability regimes, operational resilience, consumer duty, model-risk practice, and evidence gathering even without one omnibus insurance AI statute.

24.6 Australia and Singapore: Governance Before Harm

ASIC's 2024 review of 23 financial-services licensees and hundreds of AI use cases warned that governance could lag innovation and highlighted consumer and third-party risks. Singapore's FEAT principles, fairness, ethics, accountability, and transparency, and related Veritas initiatives have sought to make responsible use of AI operational in financial services.

Different legal architectures can converge on the same practical expectation: institutions should understand what their systems do before scale makes harm difficult to reverse.

24.7 International Standards and the Interoperability Strategy

NIST's voluntary AI Risk Management Framework provides a technology-and sector-agnostic structure around Govern, Map, Measure, and Manage. The Financial Stability Board focuses on macro-financial vulnerabilities such as third-party concentration, market correlation, cyber risk, and model risk. International insurance supervisory work is also evolving.

A multinational insurer should create a **regulatory interoperability matrix**: one internal control mapped to multiple external expectations. A strong Algorithmic Register, for example, can support model governance, supervisory examination, privacy records, vendor oversight, and board reporting simultaneously. Good governance is reusable.

24.8 Global Convergence Around Six Institutional Duties

The striking feature of global AI regulation is not that jurisdictions use identical rules. They do not. The striking feature is that different systems are converging around a similar set of institutional duties: accountability, fairness, explainability, meaningful human oversight, robustness, and evidence.

Read together, these regimes describe a single supervisory direction travelled at different speeds. Some jurisdictions legislate horizontally and classify by risk; some apply existing insurance law to new decision machinery; one has prescribed a statistical test. An insurer that waits to see which approach wins has misunderstood the pattern. The duties converge even where the instruments differ, and the institution that builds to the convergence, rather than to any single rulebook, will find each new regulation an exercise in mapping rather than reconstruction.

Table 24.1 Comparative Global Supervisory Expectations

Framework	Scope	Core emphasis	AIGM translation
EU AI Act	Cross-sector EU law	Risk classification; high-risk obligations	Classify legal status, then govern authority and consequence
EIOPA 2025	EU insurance supervision	Data, fairness, explainability, cyber, human oversight	Insurance-specific controls across the lifecycle
IAIS 2025	Global insurance supervision	Governance, robustness, transparency, fairness, redress	Common supervisory baseline for insurers
NAIC 2023	US state insurance model bulletin	Written AI programme; compliance with insurance law	Accountability remains with insurer
NYDFS 2024	New York underwriting and pricing	Proxy testing, discrimination, governance, disclosure	Fairness evidence and meaningful reasons
Colorado SB 21-169 and Division regulations	US state insurance law and regulation	Outcome-based unfair discrimination; prescribed governance and	Consequence regulated directly; register, owner, and evidence

		quantitative testing	required
BoE/FCA and ASIC	UK and Australia	Adoption evidence; governance pace; third parties	Operational evidence and governance maturity
NIST / FSB	Cross-sector / financial stability	Risk management; concentration; correlation; cyber	Systemic and third-party entanglement

REGIONAL INTERLUDE

The Gulf as a Governance Laboratory

The global debate on algorithmic insurance is often written from markets where insurance institutions, data systems, consumer law and supervisory structures matured long before artificial intelligence arrived. The Gulf is different. Here, digital distribution, regulatory reform, mandatory insurance expansion and new data infrastructure are evolving at the same time. That makes the region more than a local case study. It is a governance laboratory.

The United Arab Emirates: Integrated Supervision and Fast Digitisation

The Central Bank of the UAE took over the regulatory, supervisory, licensing and enforcement functions of the insurance sector after the former Insurance Authority was merged into the CBUAE under Decretal Federal Law No. 25 of 2020. The operational merger was implemented in 2021. The practical consequence is that insurers and brokers operate under a supervisor that thinks simultaneously about prudential strength, conduct, financial crime, operational resilience and the wider financial system (CBUAE, 2021; CBUAE, 2026).

From the inside of a licensed brokerage, this matters. Technology discussions do not remain technology discussions for long. A workflow that screens a customer touches financial crime controls. A model that selects an insurer touches conduct and suitability. An automated accounting action touches books, records, authority and auditability. I have found the regulatory question is rarely, "Are you using AI?" The harder question is, "Can you show who owns the decision, how the control works, and what happens when it fails?"

A UAE Case: When Claims Data Became a Management Conversation

In one corporate medical programme we analysed more than AED 1.69 million of processed claims during the reporting period, across more than 2,500 claims. The useful part was not the dashboard itself. It was what the data changed in the conversation. Pharmacy utilisation, outpatient frequency, musculoskeletal costs, dependent spend and membership growth pointed to different interventions. A single optimisation objective would have flattened those differences into one number, usually loss ratio. The broking judgement was to preserve the story behind the number: where utilisation was clinically ordinary, where behaviour could be influenced, where benefit design mattered, and where intervention would simply shift cost to the employee.

This is a recurring danger in intelligent insurance. Once analytics become visually persuasive, the organisation can start treating the dashboard as the decision. It is not. The dashboard is evidence. The decision still has to reconcile cost, benefit adequacy, employee experience, network access and the employer's purpose in buying cover.

Saudi Arabia: A Different Regulatory Path, the Same Governance Question

Saudi Arabia established the Insurance Authority in 2023 as an independent regulator for the sector, and health-insurance responsibilities were transferred to it in March 2024. The Kingdom is simultaneously expanding insurance penetration, digitising distribution and reorganising supervision, which means algorithmic governance is arriving while the market architecture itself is still moving (Insurance Authority of Saudi Arabia, 2024).

A Saudi Case: The Cheapest Quote Was Never the Whole Answer

In a Saudi motor-fleet placement handled through a local broking context, our team prepared a multi-insurer comparison rather than a price list. That distinction matters. A ranking engine can sort premiums in milliseconds. It cannot, unless deliberately designed to do so, understand why a slightly higher quotation may be preferable because of repair conditions, deductibles, exclusions, claims handling, territorial wording, or the credibility of the insurer's response. The technical problem is easy: rank the quotes. The professional problem is harder: define what "best" means before the machine ranks anything.

This is where I think the Gulf can contribute to the global discussion. Markets in the UAE and Saudi Arabia are technologically ambitious, commercially fast and culturally relationship-driven. Those characteristics create pressure for automation, but they also preserve a strong intuition that accountability sits with a person and an institution. The opportunity is to digitise without discarding that intuition.

Takaful and the Legitimacy Question

Takaful adds another layer. Its governance tradition separates commercial effectiveness from permissibility. A practice may be profitable and still fail a normative test. That is strikingly relevant to algorithmic insurance. A variable can improve prediction and still be illegitimate. A model can reduce cost and still violate the institution's obligations to customers. The governance lesson is broader than any one religious framework: prediction does not settle permission.

The Emerging-Market Warning

Emerging markets may leap directly from limited data to alternative data, from thin branch networks to embedded distribution, and from manual underwriting to automated triage. The leap can be economically valuable. It can also make governance mistakes harder to see because there is less legacy process against which to compare them. In these markets, waiting for a perfect rulebook is not a strategy. Institutions need to choose their authority boundaries before supervisors are forced to choose them on the institution's behalf.

CHAPTER 25

The Algorithmic Assurance Function

25.1 Validation Answers Only Part of the Question

Model validation asks whether a model performs as intended under defined conditions. Algorithmic insurance governance must also ask whether the intended purpose is legitimate, whether the workflow grants appropriate authority, whether outcomes are fair, whether humans can intervene, whether explanations are usable, whether the provider is governable, and whether the system remains safe after change.

A statistically valid model can be an institutionally invalid decision process.

25.2 Four Evidence Domains

High-consequence AI should produce evidence in four domains. **Technical evidence** covers performance, robustness, drift, security, and data quality. **Decision evidence** covers purpose, authority level, DCI, HAT, explanation, and reversibility. **Outcome evidence** covers customer effects, disparity, complaints, overrides, incidents, and business performance. **Governance evidence** covers ownership, approvals, third-party controls, change history, assurance, and board reporting.

The model file is therefore only one part of the assurance dossier.

25.3 The Role of Control Functions

Risk management should own the enterprise framework and challenge consequence classification. Compliance should test legal, conduct, fairness, disclosure, and redress obligations. Actuarial functions should challenge insurance relevance, pricing, reserving, and model assumptions where within mandate. Information security should test adversarial and access risk. Internal audit should assess whether the governance system works as represented.

Independent validation can sit in risk, actuarial, analytics, or a specialised function depending on structure. Independence matters more than organisational fashion.

25.4 Assurance Claims

Checklists encourage completion. **Assurance claims** encourage evidence. A system owner should make explicit statements such as: "The model does not use prohibited data directly or through material proxies"; "High-consequence adverse decisions receive effective human review"; "The vendor cannot change a material model without notification"; "Customer challenges can reverse erroneous decisions within defined service levels."

Assurance then asks: what evidence would make this claim credible, and what evidence could falsify it? This is more rigorous than asking whether a policy document exists.

25.5 Continuous Assurance

Dynamic systems require monitoring after deployment. Drift, prompt changes, new vendor versions, population shifts, changing regulation, user workarounds, and accumulated feedback can alter risk. Assurance should therefore include event-driven triggers and periodic review.

The approval date should never become the last serious governance date.

25.6 Assurance Is a Claim About a Decision System

Assurance is often described as 'testing the model'. That language is too narrow for algorithmic insurance. The assurance claim should be about the decision system: that a defined class of decisions operates within approved authority, produces evidence sufficient for challenge, remains inside fairness and security tolerances, and fails safely when uncertainty exceeds its boundaries.

This shifts assurance from a one-time technical event to an institutional claim that must remain true in production. Model validation may establish discrimination, calibration, robustness, or predictive performance. It does not prove that the right version is deployed, that workflow has not increased practical authority, that a third-party dependency remains available, that customers receive usable reasons, or that human reviewers can disagree.

A strong assurance report should therefore state its scope in decision terms. 'We validated Model X' is weaker than 'We obtained reasonable assurance that automated low-value motor claims within the defined Safe Automation Envelope are processed using approved data and model versions, are referred when specified conditions arise, remain reversible until payment, and are monitored for material outcome disparity.' The second claim can be challenged because it is specific.

Continuous assurance does not mean continuous audit. It means that selected control evidence is observed continuously and that predefined changes trigger deeper review. Deployment version, override rates, complaint reversals, fairness indicators, vendor changes, prompt changes, and authority drift can all serve as triggers.

The assurance function becomes most valuable when it is willing to narrow confidence. A carefully qualified conclusion is stronger than a broad statement of 'responsible AI' that cannot be evidenced.

25.7 Who Is Actually Able to Do This Work

Assurance frameworks are easier to design than to staff, and the staffing question determines whether the framework produces challenge or paperwork.

Three capabilities have to be present somewhere, and they rarely sit in one person. Insurance judgement, to know whether a decision is appropriate for the product, the customer, and the regulatory context. Technical literacy, sufficient to read a validation report critically and to recognise when a test does not measure what it claims to measure. And organisational standing, meaning the seniority and reporting line to say that a system should not proceed, and to have that survive contact with a delivery deadline.

The third is the one institutions most often neglect, and it is decisive. A validator who reports to the executive whose programme is being validated is producing an opinion with a known conclusion. Independence is not achieved by writing the word into a policy. It is achieved through a reporting line, a budget, and a record of findings that were unwelcome and stood anyway.

Most insurers already hold the first two capabilities inside actuarial, model risk, and internal audit functions. What they usually lack is a mandate connecting those functions to decisions rather than to models. Building a separate algorithmic assurance department is rarely the answer. Giving existing independent functions explicit authority over decision systems, and the technical support to exercise it, usually is.

25.8 Assurance Evidence Has a Shelf Life

Evidence ages, and the framework should say so rather than leaving each function to assume otherwise.

Some evidence is durable. A purpose statement, a data legitimacy assessment, or a decision-owner assignment remains valid until the underlying decision changes. Some evidence decays predictably: performance testing, drift monitoring, and fairness measurement all describe a population that moves. And some evidence is invalidated by a single event, including a model version change, a new data source, a widened eligibility rule, entry to a new jurisdiction, or a vendor's unilateral update.

A useful discipline is to record, for each material system, the date of the evidence and the condition that would void it. That converts assurance from a calendar exercise into a state the institution can query. It also exposes a common and uncomfortable finding: the systems with the highest consequence are frequently the ones whose evidence is oldest, because they were approved early, approved carefully, and then left alone.

The annual question worth asking of every Band C and Band D system is therefore not whether it was assured, but whether anything has happened since that would have changed the conclusion

CHAPTER 26

The Algorithmic Governance Charter

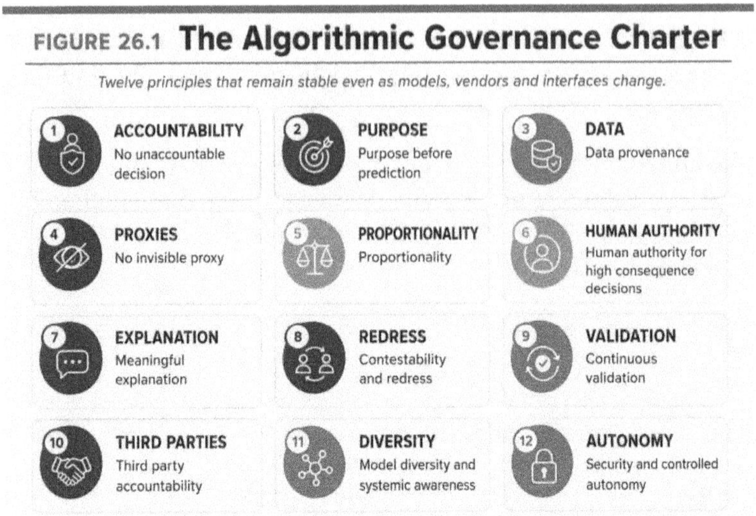

Figure 26.1. The Algorithmic Governance Charter.

26.1 Rules Change Faster Than Principles

Models, vendors, and technical methods will change faster than any book or regulation. Governance therefore needs a durable layer above tool-specific rules: a small set of principles that remain intelligible when the technology changes. Algorithmic insurance needs such a charter because delegated machine authority creates questions that a model policy cannot settle on its own.

The purpose is not poetic. Principles provide a standard for decisions that policy writers did not anticipate.

26.2 The Twelve Principles

The Algorithmic Governance Charter contains twelve principles.

1. **No Unaccountable Decision.** Every material algorithmic decision must remain attributable to accountable human institutions and named owners.
2. **Purpose Before Prediction.** Predictive power does not justify a use unless the insurance purpose is legitimate and explicit.
3. **Data Provenance.** Material data and generated evidence must be traceable, challengeable, and governed according to origin and transformation.
4. **No Invisible Proxy.** Institutions must test whether apparently neutral data or features reproduce distinctions that cannot be justified directly.
5. **Proportionality.** Governance intensity must rise with authority, consequence, vulnerability, opacity, scale, and irreversibility.
6. **Human Authority for High Consequence.** Where the Human Authority Threshold is crossed, a competent person must possess real power to change the decision.
7. **Meaningful Explanation.** Materially affected people should receive reasons they can use, not simply technical descriptions.
8. **Contestability and Redress.** People must have an effective route to correct data and challenge consequential outcomes.
9. **Continuous Validation.** Approval is not permanent; performance, drift, fairness, and workflow must be monitored after deployment.
10. **Third-Party Accountability.** Outsourcing components does not outsource the insurer's responsibility for the resulting decision.
11. **Model Diversity and Systemic Awareness.** Institutions should understand shared dependencies and avoid blind reliance on common analytical views where systemic consequences are material.
12. **Security and Controlled Autonomy.** Autonomous capability must be bounded by permissions, transaction limits, trusted inputs, escalation, and shutdown mechanisms.

26.3 Principles Can Conflict

Fairness may conflict with privacy when protected attributes are needed to test disparity. Explainability may conflict with security or intellectual property. Speed may conflict with human review. Model diversity may conflict with operational standardisation. The Charter does not eliminate these tensions. It requires them to be surfaced and governed.

A mature decision record should identify which principles are engaged, where trade-offs exist, who accepted the residual risk, and why.

26.4 From Principle to Control

A principle becomes real only when translated into evidence. No Unaccountable Decision becomes the accountability chain. Purpose Before Prediction becomes the purpose statement and Data Legitimacy Test. Proportionality becomes authority level and DCI. Human Authority becomes HAT and Effective Disagreement. Explanation becomes minimum viable explanation. Contestability becomes appeal design. Third-Party Accountability becomes dependency mapping and due diligence. Controlled Autonomy becomes permissions, limits, and kill switches.

This translation protects the principles from becoming wall posters.

26.5 The Charter Review

For Band D or Level Five systems, approval should include a short Charter Review. The decision committee walks through all twelve principles and records evidence, exceptions, conflicts, and residual risk. The review should be comprehensible to a board director, regulator, and business professional, not only to the model developer.

26.6 The Charter as a Map of Decision Rights

A charter matters because advanced AI creates a decision-rights problem. Who is allowed to delegate authority to a model? Who can increase that authority? Which decisions may never cross the HAT without explicit human judgement? Who can suspend a system when fairness evidence deteriorates?

Which responsibilities remain with the insurer when a vendor controls the model?

The twelve principles become useful when converted into rights and duties. The customer has a right to an institution that can explain and review material decisions. The board has a duty to define risk appetite for algorithmic authority. Management has a duty to maintain an inventory and assign decision owners. Control functions have a duty to challenge. Technology teams have a duty to preserve evidence and boundaries. Vendors have contractual duties to support transparency, change control, testing, and exit.

This does not make the charter a legal document. It makes it a governance architecture: a durable statement of what the institution refuses to delegate implicitly. In a fast-moving technical environment, that durability is a strength. Models will change. Interfaces will change. Agents will become more capable. The principles should remain stable enough to govern each new form without being rewritten every quarter.

CHAPTER 27

From Pilot to Institution: The Implementation Roadmap

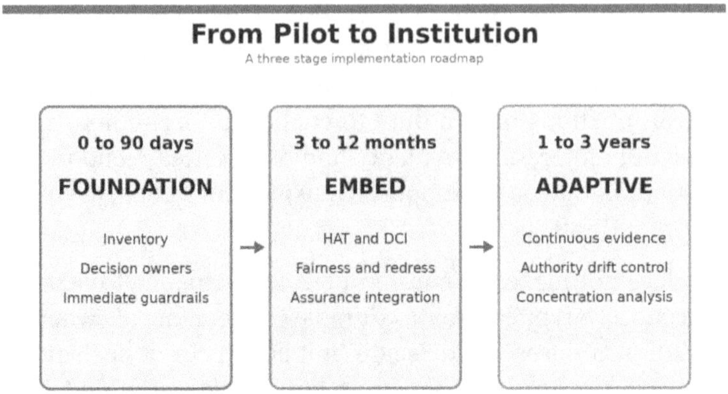

Figure 27.1. From pilot to institution.

27.1 Governance Should Make Good Innovation Easier

Poor governance slows innovation because every project renegotiates the same questions. Strong governance creates reusable pathways: known authority levels, consequence bands, templates, review thresholds, vendor standards, monitoring requirements, and escalation rules. Teams can move quickly because the institution has already decided how evidence should scale with risk.

The objective is not maximum control. It is **proportionate certainty**.

27.2 The First 90 Days, Foundation

The first ninety days should produce five outcomes. First, appoint executive and board ownership. Second, define AI broadly enough to capture material automated decision systems, not simply fashionable models. Third, build an initial Algorithmic Register by surveying business, technology, procurement, vendors, and control functions. Fourth, classify the highest-consequence systems using AIGM and DCI. Fifth, impose interim guardrails for prohibited uses, sensitive data, high-consequence autonomous decisions, public generative tools, and unapproved vendor integrations.

Do not wait for a perfect inventory before governing the obvious critical systems.

27.3 The First 12 Months, Embed

Within twelve months, the institution should establish the accountability chain, HAT rules, Data Legitimacy Test, Fairness Evidence Packs, vendor AI due diligence, model and generative validation standards, incident taxonomy, explanation and contestability standards, board dashboard, staff training, and independent assurance plan.

New projects should enter through the framework by default. Existing high-consequence systems should be remediated in priority order.

27.4 Three Years, Adaptive Governance

Mature governance is not a larger policy library. It is evidence integrated into operations. The Algorithmic Register is connected to architecture and procurement. Changes automatically trigger reassessment. Customer challenges feed monitoring. Third-party concentration is visible. Scenario exercises test autonomous systems. The board sees portfolio trends. Regulatory mapping is maintained. Business teams understand that AI authority is part of ordinary delegated authority.

By this stage, the institution should be capable of governing technology it has not yet encountered because the principles are decision-based.

27.5 The Five-Level Maturity Model

The **Algorithmic Governance Maturity Model** has five levels.

Level 1, Experimental: fragmented pilots, incomplete inventory, reliance on individual judgement.

Level 2, Controlled: basic policy, approvals, security, and model validation exist, but business integration is uneven.

Level 3, Governed: authority classification, consequence scoring, accountability, vendor controls, fairness, explanation, monitoring, and board reporting are consistent.

Level 4, Assured: independent evidence tests whether governance claims are true; incidents and customer outcomes drive improvement.

Level 5, Adaptive: governance responds dynamically to model, data, vendor, regulatory, and systemic change while preserving clear institutional principles.

27.6 The Critical Path Is Cultural

The hardest implementation barrier is rarely a missing template. It is incentive. If teams are rewarded only for automation rate, speed, expense reduction, or conversion, governance becomes a cost centre. If leaders reward justified referral, meaningful disagreement, early incident reporting, and responsible withdrawal, people learn that control quality is part of performance.

The institution will automate according to what it celebrates.

27.7 The Operating Model: Who Does What on Monday Morning?

Implementation fails when organisations treat AI governance as a policy project. The policy is necessary, but the operating model determines whether governance survives contact with delivery. Someone must own the inventory. Someone must score consequence. Someone must decide whether a workflow crosses the HAT. Someone must monitor drift. Someone must have authority to stop deployment. Someone must report exceptions to the board.

The first stage is therefore visibility. In the first 90 days, the institution should identify material AI use cases, classify practical authority, establish named decision owners, and stop any deployment where accountability cannot be reconstructed. Perfection is not required. A credible inventory is.

The second stage is integration. During the first year, HAT, DCI, fairness evidence, third-party dependency mapping, security testing, and redress evidence should be embedded into existing governance forums rather than built as a parallel AI bureaucracy. Underwriting committees should govern algorithmic underwriting. Claims committees should govern claims automation. Model risk, conduct, compliance, cyber, and operational resilience should contribute through their existing mandates.

The third stage is adaptation. Mature institutions monitor authority drift, automate selected assurance evidence, test agentic boundaries, analyse complaints and overrides as learning data, and benchmark provider concentration. Governance becomes part of how AI products are designed, not a checkpoint imposed after they are built.

The objective is not slower innovation. It is shorter uncertainty. Teams should know in advance what evidence is required for a Level Two recommendation, a Level Four execution system, or a high-DCI customer decision. Clear governance reduces the late-stage surprises that make responsible innovation slow.

Table 27.1 From Pilot to Institution: Three-Stage Implementation Roadmap

Stage	Time horizon	Priority outcomes	Evidence of maturity
Foundation	0-90 days	Inventory; authority level; decision owners; immediate stop criteria	Material use cases visible and accountable
Embed	3-12 months	HAT, DCI, fairness, vendor mapping, redress, security and assurance integrated	Governance operates through normal business forums
Adaptive	1-3 years	Continuous evidence; authority-drift monitoring; agentic controls; concentration analysis	Governance changes with the system before incidents force change

CHAPTER 28

The Human Professional After AI

28.1 The Wrong Question Is "Will AI Replace Me?"

Every major technology wave generates the same anxiety. The more useful question is: *Which parts of my work become cheap, fast, and abundant, and which parts become more valuable because machines can now do the first set?*

Insurance contains enormous amounts of search, extraction, comparison, drafting, calculation, classification, and routine communication. Much of that will become increasingly automated. Professional value will migrate toward the boundary where evidence is incomplete, objectives conflict, wording is ambiguous, people are vulnerable, systems disagree, and responsibility must be accepted.

28.2 The Underwriter Becomes a Boundary Designer

The underwriter of the future may spend less time collecting information and more time deciding where automation stops, how exceptions are interpreted, how new risks fit imperfect categories, and how portfolio signals should be challenged. The best underwriters will understand models without becoming subordinate to them.

Judgement will become more visible specifically because routine judgement becomes automated.

28.3 The Claims Professional Becomes an Advocate for the Promise

Automation can remove administrative burden from claims. Human value then concentrates in complex coverage, negotiation, empathy after severe loss, vulnerable customers, fraud judgement, disputed causation, and recovery strategy. A professional who merely moves documents will be threatened by AI. A professional who understands the promise and can resolve ambiguity becomes more valuable.

28.4 The Broker Becomes an Interpreter of Machines and Markets

Brokers will use AI to analyse wordings, benchmark markets, prepare submissions, and compare quotations. Their differentiating value will be understanding what the comparison misses: claims behaviour, market appetite, wording nuance, negotiation, client strategy, and the consequences of exclusions across a risk ecosystem.

The broker also becomes an algorithmic advocate: asking insurers how automated underwriting, claims, or pricing decisions can be explained and challenged on behalf of clients.

28.5 The Actuary and Data Scientist Gain a Social Mandate

Technical professionals will increasingly shape access, price, capital, and claims through model design. Their role therefore expands beyond statistical competence. They need fluency in purpose, fairness, uncertainty, explanation, governance, and the limits of data. Professional codes will matter more, not less, as models gain authority.

28.6 The Most Valuable Human Skill Is Responsible Disagreement

In an automated environment, agreeing with the machine is easy. The scarce skill is knowing when not to. Responsible disagreement requires domain knowledge, courage, evidence, and institutional permission. Organisations should train and reward it.

The professional future of insurance is not a contest between people and machines. It is a contest between institutions that combine them wisely and institutions that automate faster than they learn to govern.

28.7 Human Work at the Boundary

The final proposition of this book can now be stated fully: **human value moves to the boundary**, between covered and uncovered, certain and uncertain, fair and merely predictive, reversible and irreversible, routine and exceptional, institution and customer, model and world.

Those boundaries are where insurance has always required judgement. AI will not remove them. It will make them more important.

28.8 The Profession Must Stay Capable of Saying No

A profession earns trust partly through the decisions it refuses to automate. That does not mean protecting human work for sentimental reasons. It means recognising that some forms of judgement are valuable specifically because they include moral responsibility, contextual interpretation, negotiation, and the capacity to resist a technically persuasive answer.

The risk of an AI-rich profession is not only deskilling through job loss. It is deskilling through non-use. An underwriter who never prices a difficult risk without a recommendation may gradually lose the ability to recognise when the recommendation is absurd. A claims professional who rarely constructs an independent coverage view may become excellent at reviewing outputs while losing the craft needed to challenge them. A broker who relies on automated comparisons may stop noticing the wording difference that changes a client's recovery after a major loss.

Organisations should therefore preserve deliberate zones of human practice. High-consequence exceptions should be reviewed by professionals who remain capable of forming an independent judgement. Training should include cases where the model is intentionally wrong. Junior staff should learn how the conclusion is built, not simply how to operate the system that delivers it. Senior professionals should be measured partly on the quality of challenge they create in others.

This is a different view of productivity. The goal is not to maximise the percentage of decisions made without humans. It is to minimise the amount of human attention wasted on work that does not require human judgement, while protecting enough human depth for the cases that do. A mature institution automates routine cognition so that professional cognition can become more concentrated, not more superficial.

The ability to say no also belongs to the institution itself. There will be systems that are accurate, efficient, and commercially attractive but inappropriate for a particular decision because the evidence is too intrusive, the consequence too severe, the explanation too weak, the dependency too concentrated, or the human authority too thin. Governance is the discipline that gives an organisation the confidence to refuse those deployments before an incident forces the lesson.

That may ultimately be the professional advantage of the human insurance practitioner in an age of machine intelligence. The machine can calculate what follows from the assumptions it is given. The professional must still decide whether the assumptions, the boundary, and the consequence deserve to be accepted at all.

The Last Decision Must Still Be Ours

Insurance has always been an institutional answer to uncertainty. It gathers evidence about a future no one can know, converts that evidence into prices and promises, and then asks society to trust that those promises will still mean something when loss arrives.

Artificial intelligence changes the speed, scale, and texture of that work. It can read more documents than any underwriter, compare more patterns than any claims handler, simulate more scenarios than any board, and communicate with millions of customers without sleep. It can make insurance cheaper to operate, easier to buy, faster to service, more precise in risk selection, more responsive in claims, and more intelligent in prevention.

Those possibilities are real. They are also incomplete.

The central mistake would be to imagine that better prediction settles the questions insurance exists to answer. It does not. Prediction can tell us what may happen. It cannot by itself tell us what distinctions are legitimate, what protection should remain available, which errors society is willing to tolerate, when a vulnerable person deserves a human hearing, how far an institution should optimise profit against fairness, or who must stand behind a decision when the machine is wrong.

Those are questions of authority.

This book began with a simple proposition: artificial intelligence becomes a governance problem at the moment prediction becomes authority. Twenty-eight chapters later, that proposition can be stated more specifically. Algorithmic insurance is legitimate when authority is visible, proportionate, attributable, contestable, reversible where possible, and bounded by human institutions that remain capable of saying no.

The frameworks in this book exist to make those conditions operational: to locate authority before it drifts, to weigh consequence before automation is approved, to keep responsibility attached to a named person when a decision passes through many hands, and to leave an affected customer something they can actually challenge

None of these tools is offered as a final scientific formula. They are governance instruments: structured ways to make hidden assumptions visible and to force institutions to answer questions before an adverse outcome answers them on their behalf.

The Danger Is Not Intelligence

A machine does not become dangerous merely because it is intelligent. A calculator can be more accurate than a person. A fraud model can identify patterns that human investigators miss. A generative system can summarise a complex file brilliantly. A catastrophe model can reveal accumulation no individual underwriter could see.

The danger emerges when three conditions combine: the system has authority, the consequence is material, and accountability is weak.

A mediocre algorithm with little authority can be harmless. A brilliant algorithm with poorly bounded authority can be dangerous specifically because people trust it.

This is why the future cannot be governed by asking whether AI is "good" or "bad." The correct question is always more specific: *What is this system allowed to do, to whom, on what evidence, subject to what challenge, and with whose responsibility?*

The Profession Is Not Becoming Less Human

There is a paradox at the centre of automation. As machines perform more routine cognition, the remaining human work becomes more deeply human.

Someone must decide what fairness means when fairness metrics disagree. Someone must negotiate an ambiguous clause after a catastrophic loss. Someone must tell a family why an application was declined and decide whether the evidence justifies another review. Someone must decide whether the protection gap created by precise pricing is commercially rational but socially unacceptable. Someone must challenge a model that everyone else trusts. Someone must accept residual risk on behalf of the institution.

Those tasks are not leftovers after automation. They are the centre of professional responsibility.

Insurance has sometimes undervalued them because administrative work occupied so much professional time. AI can remove some of that burden. If the industry uses the opportunity wisely, it can restore professional judgement to the place it should always have occupied.

The Institution Must Be Able to Explain Itself

The most important test of algorithmic insurance may be surprisingly simple.

Imagine a customer, regulator, board director, judge, broker, or employee asking: Why did this happen?

A governed institution should be able to answer without hiding behind mathematics, software vendors, or organisational complexity. It should be able to identify the decision, the evidence, the model role, the human authority, the reasons, the route to challenge, the owner, and the corrective action if the result is wrong.

The answer does not need to reveal every parameter. It needs to reveal enough institutional reasoning to make accountability real.

When an insurer cannot explain itself because too many layers of automation stand between the customer and responsibility, the problem is not simply explainability. The institution has lost sight of its own authority.

The Systemic Question

In Insurance Risk Ecosystem Entanglement, I argued that risk is increasingly entangled. Here I extend that argument from risks to decisions. If insurers use the same data, cloud providers, models, foundation-model infrastructure, catastrophe views, and optimisation targets, the market can become cognitively entangled. A model error need not remain within one company. An analytical fashion can become a market behaviour.

The future regulator will therefore need to look beyond whether each firm's model is individually sound. The future board will need to ask whether its analytical independence is real. The future insurer will need to know not only where its risks accumulate, but where its **judgement** accumulates.

That may become one of the defining governance questions of the next decade.

A Final Charter Principle

If one principle were added above the twelve in the Algorithmic Governance Charter, it would be this:

> **Technology may extend the institution's intelligence. It must never dissolve the institution's responsibility.**

The insurer remains responsible for the promise. The broker remains responsible for professional advice. The board remains responsible for the authority it delegates. The regulator remains responsible for the market it supervises. The human professional remains responsible for knowing when the machine has reached the boundary of what it can legitimately decide.

Machines can calculate the premium.

Machines can rank the claim.

Machines can draft the explanation.

Machines can search the market.

Machines may increasingly negotiate and execute.

But the final decision about what insurance is *for*, what treatment is *fair*, what authority is *acceptable*, and what responsibility the institution is prepared to carry must still be ours.

That is not a limitation on artificial intelligence.

It is the condition under which artificial intelligence becomes worthy of trust.

AI Use-Case Inventory Template

The Algorithmic Register should be broad enough to capture conventional predictive models, rules-based automation, generative systems, embedded vendor features, and autonomous agents when they materially influence an insurance decision. The following template can be implemented in a governance platform, spreadsheet, model inventory, or enterprise architecture repository.

For every use case, record the following fields.

Identification

- Use-case ID and system name.
- Business unit and process.
- Product, line of business, and jurisdictions affected.
- Executive sponsor, decision owner, model/system owner, data owner,

and independent assurance owner.

- Internal development, external vendor, or hybrid.

Purpose and Decision

- Plain-language business purpose.
- Insurance decision affected.
- Customer, employee, intermediary, counterparty, or portfolio population

affected.

AIGM authority level: Assist, Recommend, Decide, Execute, Autonomous.

- Decision Consequence Index score and band.
- Entanglement rating and material shared dependencies.
- Human Authority Threshold and referral rules.

Technology

- Model family or technique in plain language.
- Model and software version.
- Foundation model, cloud, API, or external service dependencies.
- Tools and system permissions available to agents.

- Prompt or configuration version for generative systems.

Data

- Primary data sources.
- External consumer data used.
- Sensitive or protected characteristics directly used for lawful purposes, if

any.

- Proxy-risk assessment.
- Data Legitimacy Test status.
- Retention and correction mechanism.
- Synthetic data use and provenance.

Controls

- Validation date and approving body.
- Fairness Evidence Pack status.
- Minimum Viable Explanation design.
- Customer contestability channel.
- Human-review competence standard.
- Security and adversarial testing status.
- Transaction or execution limits.
- Kill-switch and fallback owner.

Monitoring

- Accuracy or performance measures.
- Outcome and fairness measures.
- Drift indicators.
- Override and disagreement indicators.
- Complaints, appeals, and reversal rates.
- Incidents and near misses.
- Vendor change notifications.
- Next scheduled review and event-driven triggers.

Minimum Inventory Rule

If a business unit cannot complete the fields concerning the decision affected, authority level, consequence, owner, and customer redress, the use case is not sufficiently understood to receive material decision authority.

Inventory Quality Test

Once per year, compare the Algorithmic Register with five independent sources: procurement contracts, architecture records, software inventories, data-provider payments, and staff surveys. Differences are a governance metric. A register that depends entirely on voluntary self-reporting will almost always understate embedded AI.

Human Authority Threshold Assessment

Score each factor from 0 to 4. The score is a structured trigger for governance discussion, not a substitute for law or professional judgement.

Human Authority Threshold Scoring Matrix

Factor	0	1	2	3	4
Consequence	No material external effect	Minor inconvenienc e	Moderate financial or service effect	Material coverage or financial effect	Severe rights, health, livelihood, or systemic effect
Reversibility	Immediate and complete	Easy correction	Correctable with some burden	Difficult or delayed correction	Practically irreversible
Vulnerability	Sophisticated internal user	Commercial professional	Ordinary retail customer	Financially dependent or distressed	Highly vulnerable or urgent dependency
Opacity	Direct rule	Simple interpretable model	Moderate complexity	Complex or third-party	Adaptive, opaque, and hard to reconstruct
Scale	One internal user	Small population	Product segment	Large portfolio	Market or system-wide
Time sensitivity	No time consequence	Low	Moderate	High	Delay itself may cause serious harm

Suggested Interpretation

- **0-5:** Human authority may be retrospective if the decision is reversible and law permits.
- **6-11:** Defined human referral and monitoring should exist.
- **12-17:** Pre-decision human authority should generally apply to materially adverse outcomes unless a documented safe automation envelope is approved.
- **18-24:** Critical human authority is expected. Fully autonomous adverse action should be exceptional, evidence-heavy, and board-visible.

Effective Disagreement Test

Where human oversight is claimed, answer yes or no:

1. Does the reviewer see the material evidence, not only the model recommendation?
2. Does the reviewer understand the model's purpose and known limitations?
3. Does the reviewer possess domain competence to make the decision independently?
4. Can the reviewer change the outcome without extraordinary escalation?
5. Is sufficient time allowed for meaningful review?
6. Is disagreement free from productivity penalties or cultural stigma?
7. Are overrides analysed for quality rather than merely minimised?
8. Can the reviewer escalate suspected model or data defects? A process with several “no” answers should not be represented as meaningful human oversight.

Decision Consequence Index

The Decision Consequence Index (DCI) scores six dimensions from 0 to 4, producing a total from 0 to 24. It should be completed by the business decision owner with challenge from risk or compliance. Technical teams should contribute evidence but should not determine consequence alone.

Dimension 1, Financial Impact

0: negligible. 1: small and bounded. 2: meaningful to an individual or unit. 3: material individual or portfolio effect. 4: potentially severe individual, capital, or systemic effect.

Dimension 2, Coverage and Rights Impact

0: no contractual effect. 1: convenience or internal routing. 2: affects terms or service materially. 3: affects eligibility, premium, investigation, or significant settlement. 4: decline, cancellation, major coverage restriction, denial, or equivalent rights effect.

Dimension 3, Reversibility

0: instant and harmless rollback. 1: simple correction. 2: correction creates moderate cost or delay. 3: difficult to restore position fully. 4: lost opportunity, serious delay, or other practically irreversible harm.

Dimension 4, Vulnerability

0: expert internal user. 1: sophisticated commercial counterparty. 2: ordinary customer. 3: distressed or dependent customer. 4: highly vulnerable person, urgent loss, or decision involving health, shelter, livelihood, or essential protection.

Dimension 5, Scale and Systemic Reach

0: isolated internal case. 1: small team or pilot. 2: defined segment. 3: high-volume product or large portfolio. 4: enterprise, market, or infrastructure-level reach.

Dimension 6, Opacity and Contest Difficulty

0: transparent deterministic rule. 1: simple model with clear reason codes. 2: moderate complexity with reconstructable explanation. 3: complex vendor or ensemble with limited transparency. 4: adaptive, agentic, or highly opaque system with difficult evidence reconstruction.

Decision Bands

- **Band A: 0-5, Low consequence.** Standard technology and data controls may be sufficient.
- **Band B: 6-11, Moderate.** Formal owner, validation, monitoring, and referral controls required.
- **Band C: 12-17, High.** Strong fairness, explanation, HAT, independent assurance, and board or executive visibility.
- **Band D: 18-24, Critical.** Exceptional evidence burden, explicit residual-risk acceptance, strong human reservation, scenario testing, and constrained authority.

DCI Review Triggers

Rescore when the system gains new tool permissions, moves to a new customer population, enters a new jurisdiction, changes from recommendation to automatic action, increases transaction limits, adopts a new foundation model or material vendor, changes its target variable, or experiences a material incident.

Algorithmic Incident Severity Scale

An algorithmic incident is any event in which an AI-enabled or automated decision system materially departs from expected, authorised, fair, secure, or explainable operation. The definition should include near misses.

Level 1, Anomaly

A contained error or unexpected output with no external consequence. Examples: incorrect internal summary caught before use; temporary retrieval failure; isolated non-material hallucination.

Required response: record in model/system monitoring; correct; evaluate recurrence.

Level 2, Control Failure

A control fails but external harm is absent or minor. Examples: unapproved prompt change; missed monitoring threshold; limited unauthorised data use; small number of incorrect customer messages quickly corrected.

Required response: owner investigation, control remediation, compliance notification where relevant, trend analysis.

Level 3, Material Customer or Business Impact

Multiple customers or material operations are affected, or a high-consequence decision is wrong. Examples: systematic claim delays, pricing error, incorrect declinatures, significant vendor-model degradation.

Required response: incident team, stop/limit authority, customer remediation, root-cause analysis, executive notification, regulatory assessment.

Level 4, Major Event

Large-scale unfair outcomes, serious rights or financial harm, major security compromise, significant capital or portfolio effect, or sustained inability to explain critical decisions.

Required response: executive crisis governance, board notification, regulator engagement where required, independent review, broad remediation, model suspension or rollback.

Level 5, Systemic or Catastrophic Algorithmic Event

Enterprise or market-wide consequences, severe autonomous action, widespread customer harm, critical infrastructure dependency failure, or correlated model behaviour capable of threatening market function.

Required response: board-led crisis governance, immediate authority withdrawal where feasible, supervisory coordination, systemic impact assessment, independent investigation, public communication as appropriate, and formal lessons-learned programme.

Near-Miss Rule

A near miss should be classified according to the consequence that reasonably could have occurred, not the consequence that happened by luck. A payment agent stopped seconds before an erroneous large transfer is not a Level 1 event merely because the money did not leave.

APPENDIX E

Third-Party AI Due-Diligence Questionnaire

The following questions are designed for material AI providers. Not every low-risk software feature requires the full questionnaire. The burden should follow AIGM authority and DCI consequence.

Governance and Ownership

1. Who is accountable for the service and its model-risk governance?
2. Which material subcontractors, cloud providers, model providers, and data providers support the service?
3. Can any of those dependencies change without customer notification?
4. What regulatory examinations, independent audits, or assurance reports are available?

Model and Data

5. What is the intended purpose and known unsuitable use?
6. What model families are used and how are versions controlled?
7. What categories of training and validation data were used?
8. How is data provenance documented?
9. What prohibited or sensitive data controls exist?
10. What testing has been performed for unfair or disparate outcomes?
11. Can customer-specific errors in source data be corrected and propagated?

Performance and Change

12. What performance measures are monitored in production?
13. How is drift detected?
14. What changes can the provider make unilaterally?
15. What notice is provided before a material model, prompt, policy, or data-source change?
16. Can the insurer pin or roll back versions?

Explainability and Evidence

17. What evidence can be provided for an individual output?
18. Are reason codes stable and meaningful in insurance terms?
19. Can the provider support regulatory or customer challenge without disclosing unnecessary intellectual property?
20. How long are logs and generation evidence retained?

Security and Autonomy

21. How are prompt injection, data poisoning, model extraction, and adversarial inputs tested?
22. What tool permissions can an agent exercise?
23. Are transaction limits and allow-lists configurable by the insurer?
24. How is privileged access separated?
25. Is a kill switch available and who can invoke it?

Operational Resilience

26. What are recovery time and recovery point capabilities?
27. What manual or alternate-service fallback is supported?
28. Can data, configuration, prompts, embeddings, and records be exported on exit?
29. How long would realistic migration take?
30. How are critical incidents notified and investigated?

Contractual Governance

31. Does the insurer have audit and testing rights proportionate to consequence?
32. Are material model changes a defined contractual event?
33. Is cooperation with regulators required?
34. Are data-use rights limited to agreed purposes?
35. Does the contract preserve the insurer's ability to explain, contest, remediate, and exit?

Decision Rule

For a Band C or D use case, inability to obtain sufficient evidence should reduce the authority granted to the provider's output. Procurement convenience is not a control substitute.

Board Algorithmic Governance Dashboard

A board dashboard should be concise enough to govern and detailed enough to reveal change. Suggested quarterly sections follow.

1. Portfolio of Algorithmic Authority

- Total registered systems.
- Systems by AIGM Level 1-5.
- Systems by DCI Bands A-D.
- Number of Band C/D systems with Level 3+ authority.
- New deployments, material changes, and retirements.

2. Customer and Decision Outcomes

- Automated acceptance, decline, referral, and payment volumes.
- Complaint and challenge rates for AI-influenced decisions.
- Percentage of challenges resulting in changed outcomes.
- Fairness indicators and unexplained disparities.
- Vulnerable-customer effects.
- Material explanation failures.

3. Human Authority

- Override rates by high-consequence use case.
- Quality review of overrides.
- Teams with unusually low disagreement.
- HAT exceptions and temporary waivers.
- Training and competence coverage.

4. Model and Data Health

- Drift thresholds breached.
- Material data-quality incidents.
- Model version changes.
- Synthetic-data use in critical models.
- Validation findings overdue.

5. Third-Party and Systemic Dependency

- Top model, cloud, and data dependencies by decision consequence.
- Concentration appetite exceptions.
- Critical vendor incidents.
- Exit tests completed.
- Model Monoculture Factor for major portfolio decisions.

6. Security and Autonomous Systems

- Adversarial-testing findings.
- Prompt-injection or agent-permission incidents.
- Level Five autonomous systems and transaction limits.
- Kill-switch tests.
- Privileged tool-access changes.

7. Assurance and Regulation

- Open high-risk assurance findings.
- Regulatory changes and implementation status.
- Internal-audit issues.
- Material incidents by severity level.
- Charter Review exceptions.

Board Questions

Every dashboard should end with three explicit questions requiring board judgement, not simply noting: What authority has increased this quarter? Where is the organisation most dependent on evidence it cannot independently verify? Which automated decision would be hardest to explain publicly if it failed tomorrow?

Five-Level AI Governance Maturity Model

Level 1, Experimental

AI adoption is decentralised. Inventory is incomplete. Governance depends on project teams. Vendor features can appear without formal reassessment. Human oversight is described informally. Incidents are handled as technology problems.

Evidence of Level 1: different functions report different AI inventories; no common authority classification; generative AI use grows through employee experimentation; board reporting is episodic.

Level 2, Controlled

The organisation has an AI policy, basic approval process, security standards, model validation, and named programme leadership. High-profile use cases receive review, but embedded automation and third-party features may remain inconsistent.

Evidence of Level 2: central committee exists; model-risk tiers are used; procurement has AI questions; gaps remain between policy and workflow.

Level 3, Governed

The Algorithmic Register is reasonably complete. AIGM authority, DCI, HAT, accountability, data legitimacy, fairness, explanation, contestability, vendor controls, change triggers, and board reporting operate consistently for material systems.

Evidence of Level 3: business decision owners are named; controls scale by consequence; customer challenge data enters monitoring; high-consequence changes automatically trigger reassessment.

Level 4, Assured

Independent functions test whether governance claims are actually true. Outcome evidence, incidents, near misses, human disagreement, fairness, vendor concentration, and security testing are integrated. The board receives exception-focused reporting.

Evidence of Level 4: assurance can falsify first-line claims; scenario exercises test critical automation; external providers are subject to evidence-based challenge; remediation is tracked to outcome.

Level 5, Adaptive

The governance system responds to changing models, data, regulation, vendors, market behaviour, and autonomous capability without constant redesign. Principles remain stable while controls evolve. Systemic dependencies and model monoculture are actively monitored.

Evidence of Level 5: inventory integrates with architecture and procurement; event-driven governance is automated; control thresholds adapt under formal authority; the organisation can safely withdraw or reduce algorithmic authority during stress.

Maturity Warning

Maturity is not a race to Level 5. A small insurer with limited AI may be well governed at Level 3. The objective is governance proportional to actual authority and consequence, not the largest possible control bureaucracy.

Glossary of Algorithmic Insurance Governance Terms

Algorithmic Accountability Chain (AAC). The seven-link assignment of board oversight, executive sponsorship, decision ownership, model/system ownership, data ownership, human-authority ownership, and independent assurance for a material AI use case.

Algorithmic Authority. The practical power granted to a system to assist, recommend, decide, execute, or act autonomously in an insurance process.

Algorithmic Insurance Governance Model (AIGM). The framework developed in this book that governs AI according to authority, decision consequence, human authority, accountability, explanation, and systemic dependency.

Algorithmic Insurance Risk Cube. A three-axis view of Authority Level, Decision Consequence, and Entanglement used to identify governance intensity.

Algorithmic Register. The enterprise inventory of AI-enabled and materially automated decision systems, including embedded and third-party components.

Authority Boundary. The point in a workflow at which model output acquires practical consequence over an insurance decision or action.

Authority Drift. The gradual increase of a system's practical authority through workflow integration or user reliance without an explicit model change.

Bounded Agency. The principle that autonomous systems operate within explicit limits on objectives, data, tools, value, counterparties, duration, and escalation.

Bounded Inference. The principle that an institution should govern not only which data it collects but which classes of inference it permits itself to draw.

Data Legitimacy Test. Six-question assessment of purpose, provenance, accuracy, proxy risk, reasonable expectation, and proportionality for data used in material insurance decisions.

Decision Consequence Index (DCI). A 0-24 governance heuristic scoring financial impact, rights, reversibility, vulnerability, scale/systemic reach, and opacity/contest difficulty.

Decision Lineage. The reconstructable chain from source data through transformation, model, rule, human intervention, and execution to the final insurance outcome.

Effective Disagreement Test. Assessment of whether a claimed human reviewer has information, competence, time, authority, and institutional freedom to disagree with an algorithm.

Entanglement. The degree to which risk or decision processes depend on shared infrastructure, models, data, providers, or correlated behaviour across a system.

Fairness Evidence Pack. The evidence dossier documenting population, feature legitimacy, disparity and error tests, metric choices, mitigations, residual issues, and monitoring for a high-consequence model.

Generation Evidence Record. For a consequential generative output, the retained record of request, prompt, model/version, retrieved sources, tool calls, output, human edits, action, and timestamp.

Human Authority Threshold (HAT). The point at which consequence, reversibility, vulnerability, opacity, scale, or time sensitivity requires meaningful human authority before or around an algorithmic outcome.

Human Reservation. Categories of institutional purpose, values, ambiguous fairness, and critical residual-risk decisions that remain explicitly human unless a deliberate governance decision provides otherwise.

Minimum Viable Explanation (MVE). A usable explanation containing outcome, material reasons, evidence, authority, and route to redress.

Model Monoculture Factor (MMF). A qualitative diagnostic of common analytical dependency across provider concentration, data-source overlap, architectural similarity, shared targets, and behavioural coupling.

Opportunity Fairness. The principle that materially similar customers should have reasonable opportunity to discover, understand, and access appropriate insurance options subject to legitimate differences.

Safe Automation Envelope. A defined set of cases whose evidence, consequence, fraud risk, reversibility, and limits support automated decision or execution.

Trusted Input Boundary. The distinction between authorised decision inputs and untrusted content that must not be allowed to redefine system instructions or permissions.

APPENDIX I

Research Basis and References

This book is a work of professional scholarship rather than an empirical dissertation submitted to a university. Its conceptual models are designed to be testable, criticisable, and adaptable. The AIGM, DCI, HAT, accountability chain, Algorithmic Insurance Risk Cube, Model Monoculture Factor, Minimum Viable Explanation, Safe Automation Envelope, and Algorithmic Governance Charter are proposed frameworks. They should be subjected to empirical validation, jurisdiction-specific legal review, replication, and practical refinement as evidence accumulates. Regulatory and company-specific statements are dated to the sources listed below.

Public examples are used to illustrate governance questions, not to imply criticism of an organisation beyond the public record. Corporate performance examples are described as company-reported where appropriate. Composite cases are explicitly identified.

Documented cases are used for a narrow purpose: to illuminate a governance mechanism. Company-reported operational figures are identified as such. Regulatory positions are attributed to the issuing authority. Where a case is composite, the text says so explicitly. The book does not infer misconduct beyond the public record, and it does not treat a successful technology deployment as proof that the governance model behind it is universally transferable.

The reference style is author-date. This keeps the main text readable while allowing a reader to trace the supporting source in Appendix I. The legal and regulatory landscape for artificial intelligence is moving quickly; readers should therefore treat jurisdiction-specific requirements as dated to the source cited and verify current obligations before relying on them in practice.

Core Regulation, Supervision, and Standards

Australian Securities and Investments Commission. (2024). Report 798: Beware the gap: Governance arrangements in the face of AI innovation.

Bank of England & Financial Conduct Authority. (2024). Artificial intelligence in UK financial services - 2024.

Bank of England. (2025). Financial Stability in Focus: Artificial intelligence in the financial system.

European Insurance and Occupational Pensions Authority. (2025). Opinion on artificial intelligence governance and risk management.

European Union. (2024). Regulation (EU) 2024/1689 laying down harmonised rules on artificial intelligence (Artificial Intelligence Act). Official Journal of the European Union.

Financial Stability Board. (2024). The financial stability implications of artificial intelligence.

Financial Stability Board. (2025). Monitoring adoption of artificial intelligence and related vulnerabilities in the financial sector.

International Association of Insurance Supervisors. (2025). Application Paper on the supervision of artificial intelligence.

National Association of Insurance Commissioners. (2023). Model Bulletin on the Use of Artificial Intelligence Systems by Insurers.

National Institute of Standards and Technology. (2023). Artificial Intelligence Risk Management Framework (AI RMF 1.0), NIST AI 100-1.

National Institute of Standards and Technology. (2024). Artificial Intelligence Risk Management Framework: Generative Artificial Intelligence Profile, NIST AI 600-1.

New York State Department of Financial Services. (2024). Insurance Circular Letter No. 7: Use of artificial intelligence systems and external consumer data and information sources in insurance underwriting and pricing.

Central Bank of the UAE. (2021). CBUAE commences operational procedures to execute Insurance Authority merger.

Central Bank of the UAE. (2026). Insurance Guidelines: The CBUAE approach to insurance supervision.

Colorado General Assembly. (2021). Senate Bill 21-169, Restrict Insurers' Use of External Consumer Data, codified at C.R.S. 10-3-1104.9.

Colorado Division of Insurance. (2023, as amended). Regulation 10-1-1: Governance and risk management framework requirements for insurers' use of external consumer data and information sources, algorithms, and predictive models.

European Union. (2016). Regulation (EU) 2016/679 (General Data Protection Regulation), Article 22.

European Union. (2022). Regulation (EU) 2022/2554 on digital operational resilience for the financial sector (DORA).

Insurance Authority of Saudi Arabia. (2024). Transfer of health-insurance responsibilities from the Council of Health Insurance to the Insurance Authority.

Scholarship and Foundational Reading

Bainbridge, L. (1983). Ironies of automation. Automatica, 19(6), 775-779.

Barocas, S., Hardt, M., & Narayanan, A. (2023). Fairness and Machine Learning: Limitations and Opportunities. MIT Press / fairmlbook.org.

Bender, E. M., Gebru, T., McMillan-Major, A., & Shmitchell, S. (2021). On the dangers of stochastic parrots: Can language models be too big? Proceedings of FAccT 2021.

Buolamwini, J., & Gebru, T. (2018). Gender Shades: Intersectional accuracy disparities in commercial gender classification. Proceedings of FAT* 2018.

Dietvorst, B. J., Simmons, J. P., & Massey, C. (2015). Algorithm aversion: People erroneously avoid algorithms after seeing them err. Journal of Experimental Psychology: General, 144(1), 114-126.

Koster, O., Kosman, R., & Visser, J. (2021). A checklist for explainable AI in the insurance domain. arXiv:2107.14039.

Lundberg, S. M., & Lee, S.-I. (2017). A unified approach to interpreting model predictions. Advances in Neural Information Processing Systems, 30.

Obermeyer, Z., Powers, B., Vogeli, C., & Mullainathan, S. (2019). Dissecting racial bias in an algorithm used to manage the health of populations. Science, 366(6464), 447-453.

Parasuraman, R., Sheridan, T. B., & Wickens, C. D. (2000). A model for types and levels of human interaction with automation. IEEE Transactions on Systems, Man, and Cybernetics - Part A, 30(3), 286-297.

Ribeiro, M. T., Singh, S., & Guestrin, C. (2016). Why should I trust you? Explaining the predictions of any classifier. Proceedings of KDD 2016.

Rudin, C. (2019). Stop explaining black box machine learning models for high stakes decisions and use interpretable models instead. Nature Machine Intelligence, 1, 206-215.

Sculley, D., et al. (2015). Hidden technical debt in machine learning systems. Advances in Neural Information Processing Systems, 28.

Selbst, A. D., Boyd, D., Friedler, S. A., Venkatasubramanian, S., & Vertesi, J. (2019). Fairness and abstraction in sociotechnical systems. Proceedings of FAT* 2019.

Avraham, R., Logue, K. D., & Schwarcz, D. (2014). Understanding insurance antidiscrimination laws. Southern California Law Review, 87(2), 195-274.

Barry, L., & Charpentier, A. (2020). Personalization as a promise: Can Big Data change the practice of insurance? Big Data & Society, 7(1).

Frees, E. W., & Huang, F. (2023). The discriminating (pricing) actuary. North American Actuarial Journal, 27(1), 2-24.

Prince, A. E. R., & Schwarcz, D. (2020). Proxy discrimination in the age of artificial intelligence and big data. Iowa Law Review, 105(3), 1257-1318.

Swedloff, R. (2014). Risk classification's big data (r)evolution. Connecticut Insurance Law Journal, 21(1), 339-373.

Khandani, A. E., & Lo, A. W. (2007). What happened to the quants in August 2007? Journal of Investment Management, 5(4), 29-78.

Public Cases and Industry Examples Referenced

Lemonade, Inc. (2026). Form 10-K for the fiscal year ended 31 December 2025. U.S. Securities and Exchange Commission.

Moffatt v. Air Canada, 2024 BCCRT 149 (British Columbia Civil Resolution Tribunal).

Progressive Corporation. (2026). Form 10-K for the fiscal year ended 31 December 2025. U.S. Securities and Exchange Commission.

Progressive Corporation. Snapshot usage-based insurance disclosures in 2025 annual reporting.

Public cyber-loss and market examples are used only where the mechanism is material to the governance argument; quantitative loss estimates should be verified against the cited primary source before republication.

Suggested Research Agenda

The conceptual framework in this book opens several areas suitable for doctoral, regulatory, actuarial, and interdisciplinary research:

1. Empirical validation of the Decision Consequence Index across insurance lines and jurisdictions.
2. Measurement of effective human disagreement and automation bias in underwriting and claims.

3. Quantification of model-provider concentration and the Model Monoculture Factor across insurance markets.
4. Comparative analysis of fairness metrics in risk-based pricing and claims triage.
5. Consumer comprehension testing of the Minimum Viable Explanation.
6. Longitudinal study of authority drift after AI deployment.
7. Measurement of protection-gap effects created by increasingly granular algorithmic pricing.
8. Governance design for autonomous insurance agents and machine-to-machine contracting.
9. Methods for measuring algorithmic correlation among insurers without compromising competition law.
10. Board competence and assurance models for high-consequence algorithmic insurance systems.

The field is young. That is specifically why governance concepts should be developed before institutional practice hardens around assumptions that were never consciously chosen.

INDEX

Page numbers in bold indicate the principal discussion. Terms defined in the glossary at Appendix H carry a reference to that entry.

www.ingramcontent.com/pod-product-compliance
Lightning Source LLC
LaVergne TN
LVHW050815061126
851857LV00012B/819